MESILA
Providing the Path to Financial Stability

AF885163

Mesila's Financial Literacy Course

Advanced High School Program

Educator's Guide

Sephardic Edition

MESILA
Providing The Path to Financial Stability

Adapted from Mesila's High School Program - Sephardic Edition

ISBN-13:978-1-941902-24-0

Authored by:
Malky Heimowitz
and Batya Weinberg

Questions or comments may be sent to:

Mesila
P.O.B. 57116
Jerusalem 9157002, Israel
Tel: +972.2.500.0475
Fax: +972.2.500.0478
info@mesila.org
www.mesila.org
Reg. Amuta No. 580361236
Tax ID No. 11-3597720

Please note:

This material is intended for use exclusively in the context of a Mesila-authorized course. It may not be used without prior written permission from Mesila's Jerusalem headquarters.

החוברת טעונה גניזה
Parts of this publication may require *genizah*.
Please do not discard.

Table of Contents

Units

Part 1: Units 7

Student Resources

Part 2: Student Resources 65

Assignments

Part 3: Assignments 151

Appendix

Part 4: Mesila Student Guide to Budgeting 165

Introduction

An Ounce of Prevention

The Mesila Financial Literacy Course is designed to give young people the tools to manage their finances correctly and avoid pitfalls and missteps. In Mesila's many years of working with families to achieve financial stability, we have seen that much financial stress and heartache can be avoided with preventative financial education.

As more and more U.S. states began to require personal finance courses in high schools, many Jewish schools faced a unique dilemma: on the one hand, we wish to equip our students with the tools, skills, and knowledge they will require in order to be financially literate and achieve financial stability; on the other hand, the information as presented in secular curricula is often at odds - overtly or subtly - with the educational values that Torah institutions promote. For example:

- Consumerism: In the secular world, encouraging people to purchase more is considered beneficial, since it stimulates the economy. In our worldview, however, consumerism is dangerous, because it emphasizes the material, at the expense of the spiritual.
- Wealth: Building wealth is the primary goal of secular financial literacy education. As Torah Jews, we perceive money as merely a means to an end, and do not encourage building wealth as a goal unto itself.
- Interest, loans, life insurance: These are some areas of finance that involve serious halachic issues. In presenting these topics, teachers have to be extremely sensitive to the halachic ramifications.
- Careers: Our students walk the tightrope of having to generate income without compromising Torah values such as raising a family, preserving insularity, and supporting Torah study.

In consideration of our students' unique needs and sensitivities, Mesila developed a financial literacy course teaching the relevant material through the prism of Torah hashkafah and taking into account the realities and challenges students will face. The course has been taught successfully and has been well received in high schools, seminaries, and metivtas all over the world.

The current edition of the financial literacy material comprises a more intensive and demanding college-level treatment of the subject. While addressing all the hashkafic and halachic issues mentioned above, this curriculum also deepens the students' familiarity with universal financial concepts and how they affect our economic world.

The Teachers' Guide provides a clear and concise seven-unit course outline that covers all important points, while leaving the teacher ample room for creativity and innovation in presenting the material.

Please note the following elements present in the Guide:

- Course outline: Each unit addresses one major area of financial literacy, with a sidebar on the first page summarizing the unit's goals. The body of the unit presents the issues, solutions and underlying principles in bullet list form.
- Textbook readings: Each unit contains references to readings from the textbook Personal Finance (tenth edition), by Kappor, Dlabay and Hughes (Mcgraw-Hill/ Irwin 2012). These readings are crucial in order to flesh out the basic economic concepts.
- Applications: Suggestions for practical exercises translate the theoretical material in each unit into real-life application.
- Reference to Student Resource material: At key points in each unit, the students are referred to resource materials in their student text, which include Torah sources, enlightening articles, and worksheets.. This material should not be regarded as "extra enrichment," but rather as crucial information to round out the unit.

- Powerpoint Presentations: A number of subjects, such as attitudes and credit card use, are colorfully presented in visual form via well-designed video presentations. These serve as an excellent basis for class discussion.
- Unit Assignments: The assignments at the end of each unit have been proven to be extremely effective in cementing the concepts that were covered. These may be assigned as individual or group work, or creatively presented in interactive form, such as a panel discussion or even a student fair.
- Springboards for Discussion: At some junctures in the Teachers' Guide, suggestions appear for topics that can rouse lively debate. The teacher may choose from these the ones most suitable for the class.

Due to the high level of the course, options are available for college credits. Contact the office for details.

Thanks to Mrs. Tehilla Lichtenstein, academic coordinator academic coordinator and college liaison at Meohr Bais Yaakov in Jerusalem, for her invaluable assistance and input in the preparation of this course.

Each student who benefits from Mesila education is benefiting invaluably from the wisdom and acumen of Mrs. Ita Schweitzer who's imprint has influenced every page of this work in too many ways to list.

We wish to give special thanks to Mrs. Devora Reichel for her superb editing. All of Mesila educational material is graced with the gifted style of Mrs. Feige Savitsky's graphic talent. We wish to thank them both for their invaluable assistance in all areas above and beyond the call of duty.

All of Mesila's work is blessed with the influence of founder and chairman Rabbi Shmuli Margulies whose vision of Torah-based financial literacy for Jews worldwide is our guiding inspiration.

Mesila Education Division

Note:

The Mesila Financial Literacy Course is designed to be taught in conjunction with the recommended course textbook, *Personal Finance* (tenth edition) by Jack R. Kapoor, Les R. Dlabay and Robert J. Hughes (McGraw-Hill/Irwin 2012).

Textbook readings and applications appear throughout the curriculum.

Part 1:
Units

Unit 1

Financial Stability

Goals:

- To understand what financial stability is and why it's important
- To identify obstacles to financial stability
- To examine spending habits and their impact on financial stability
- To learn how to prioritize and make financially sound decisions
- To understand the concepts of opportunity cost and the time value of money.
- To identify mistaken attitudes toward money and replace them with healthy attitudes.

A. Introduction to Financial Stability

1) Financial stability - standard definition: Having adequate income to cover your expenses, both present and future.

2) Mesila's definition: Financial stability is the ability to handle your financial obligations in a way that contributes positively to other areas of your life. If you are financially stable, then your finances should enhance - not detract from - your health, your relationships, your quality of life, your peace of mind, and your ability to reach your life goals. This definition of financial stability views money as a tool, a means to a higher end, rather than as an end unto itself.

3) Difference between the two definitions: Do we equate success with how much money we have, or with how well we live with what we have?

4) Financial instability is what happens when finances become a source of anxiety, difficulty, or strife.

5) Financial stability is not a function of how much money you have. There are millionaires who suffer from terrible financial instability, because money is a source of tension and conflict in their lives, and there are low-income families who are models of financial stability, because they manage well with what they have and lead productive, happy lives despite their meager means.

6) Obstacles to financial stability:

   There are a number of reasons why a family might experience financial difficulty:

   a) Low income: Many families simply do not earn enough money to cover basic living costs.

b) High standard of living: Some families have enough money to cover basic living costs, but spend more than they have in order to live on a higher standard. This might be due to social pressure, a desire to impress others, a desire for comfort or convenience, or habits ingrained from childhood.

c) A one-time expense: A family might experience financial difficulty because of a large one-time expense such as buying a home, the birth of a child, a wedding, or a medical procedure.

d) Reduction of income: Unemployment, a pay cut, or a family business that is doing poorly can severely reduce a family's income, leading to financial difficulty.

e) Jumbled business and personal finances: When business finances are mixed up with personal finances - i.e., the business owner's salary is used to pay business debts, while the profits of the business are used to pay for the family's expenditures - finances become chaotic. Not knowing which funds need to stay in the business and which funds belong to the family can cause the financial collapse of the business, the family, or both.

f) Misplaced piety: Some people misunderstand the concept of *bitachon* and say "Hashem will help" when proactive measures are called for.

g) Carelessness: A cavalier attitude to money is a significant contributing factor, and at times the only factor, in many cases of financial difficulty. A careless attitude towards money manifests itself in superficial management of finances and irresponsible financial behavior, such as spending or investing money wantonly without considering the ramifications or risks. People with this attitude tend to think in terms of profit, and not in terms of stability. They see lack of money as a temporary, confined problem, and try to find instant solutions instead of working hard and planning for the long-term.

h) Gambling and spending addictions: Like other addictions, gambling and spending addictions are terribly destructive, and require professional intervention. Gamblers and compulsive spenders can squander huge amounts of money and land their families in serious financial trouble.

- Student Resource no. 1: **Mesila's Guidelines for Financial Stability and Accompanying Exercise**

These 47 points, culled from Mesila's many years of experience counseling families and businesses, constitute a succinct overview of the elements of financial stability.

Reflection: Which of the points in these Guidelines for Financial Stability did you find surprising or counterintuitive? Have you ever experienced something similar to any of the scenarios in the accompanying exercise?

Discussion: Keep in mind that almost all of the scenarios in the exercise are fertile ground for heated discussion. Allow time for directed debate, while ensuring that all the scenarios are touched upon.

B. Financial Stability in Practical Terms

Having everything you need and some of what you want.

1. "Everything you need"

a) A person has to be aware of what he/she needs and wants in order to function and thrive. This is the basis of establishing spending priorities.

b) Needs are subjective, based on the following factors:

(1) Society (Location/Time): Your needs are determined, to a large extent, by the place and time you live in.

(a) If you live in Eretz Yisrael, you might consider a car a luxury. If you live in North America, you might consider a second car a necessity.

(b) To a person who was born in the 1940s, a cell phone is a nice thing to have, but it's possible to manage without it, too. To a person born in the 1990s, a cell phone might be an absolute necessity.

(c) A person's society also determines what is considered wealth. For example:

- Rothschild rode in a horse and buggy and had no indoor plumbing or air conditioning - so why did he feel like Rothschild and we don't?
- A researcher said that the time of his life when he felt the richest was when he was on assignment in Africa and his hut had a thatched roof while the other huts had simpler roofs.

(2) Personality: People have different physical needs and sensitivities.

(a) Some people can live on tuna sandwiches happily; they might not understand someone else's need to eat out when there's nothing in the fridge

(b) Some people can sleep on any type of bed; to them, it seems odd that people would invest in expensive mattresses or bedding

(3) Upbringing & Conditioning: If someone is brought up with more, they might need more than others. This reality is also reflected in halachah: One is obligated to give charity according to the lifestyle to which the needy person is accustomed, not according to an objective standard of need, because needs are not objective.

(4) Circumstances: Different circumstances give rise to different needs.

(a) Size/age of family: A large family might need a larger house or car. A young family might need a lot of babysitting.

(b) Work schedule: A mother who is working might take more household help or buy readymade food.

(c) Illness or disability: When people are not well, they may need treatments, therapies, or various types of help.

c) Student Resource no. 2 : **Maslow's Hierarchy of Needs**

There are different categories of needs, expressed as a pyramid in Maslow's Hierarchy of Needs: Physiological, safety, love/belonging, esteem, self-actualization. When establishing spending priorities, all of these needs have to be taken into account. It is important to realize, however, that many needs cannot be met with money.

2. "Some of what you want"

a) It is important to have some of what you want (but not **everything** you want) because practically speaking, a person cannot function optimally unless his needs are met and he also has a bit extra that is not absolutely necessary, so that he doesn't feel suffocated or deprived.

b) There is no limit to what a person can want. Therefore, it's important to think through your wants before deciding to indulge one, because having one thing you want often comes at the expense of something you want more. *(See next page - opportunity cost)*

Student Resource no. 3: **Fifteen Hundred Dollar Eye Glasses**

3. Differentiating between needs and wants

How do we know whether something is a need or a want?

- Needs: Generally, if needs are unmet, they become more intense and lead to feelings of deprivation.
- Wants: Generally, if we deny ourselves something we want, we exercise and strengthen our self-control and self-discipline muscles.

  Example: If a person is hungry and does not yield to the urge to eat, he will only become hungrier, because he has a real need for food. But if a person wants chocolate and does not give in to the urge, eventually his desire for chocolate will abate and it will become easier for him to resist the temptation.
- Test for differentiating between needs and wants: Wait a while and see - does the desire intensify or weaken with time? Needs tend to intensify with time and wants tend to abate.

Discussion: When standard of living rises, causing luxuries ("wants") to become necessities ("needs"), does that make people happier or less content? Give examples of wants that have become needs. Note: The incidence of depression is much higher in wealthy countries.

4. Establishing spending priorities

- What does "I can't afford it" mean? Sometimes it means you don't have the money; sometimes it means it's not important to you.
- Opportunity cost
  1. Dictionary definition: Cost in terms of foregoing alternatives
  2. Practical definition: If I buy this, I can't buy that
  3. The Time/Energy/Money Triangle:

  Human beings have three main types of resources: time, energy, and money. Every action you take and every pursuit in which you engage will require a balance of the three. Often, you can save money by expending more time or energy, or you can conserve time or energy by spending money.

5. Marshmallow Experiment

In the 1960s, psychologist Walter Mischel conducted the famous Marshmallow Temptation Study among four-year-olds. In this experiment, Mischel presented each child with a marshmallow.

He then told the child that he or she could either eat the marshmallow immediately, or wait and get an additional marshmallow as a reward.

As anticipated, some children yielded to the temptation and some others withstood it. Walter Mischel followed the progress of these children, monitored their school records, and surveyed and interviewed their teachers and parents until the students reached age 18.

Results

What he found has significant implications for education: children who had resisted the marshmallow temptation turned out to be more successful and emotionally balanced than those who had given into the temptation.

They were better-adjusted and more dependable.

More specifically, children who could delay gratification scored 250 points higher on the Scholastic Aptitude Test, worked well under pressure and when in groups, were significantly more confident, and possessed a number of other positive traits and habits.

a) It is important to emphasize that even though there are those who are born with a tendency for more restraint, the possibilities of what a person can achieve are endless, and it is our job in life to overcome negative character traits.

b) When it comes to spending money in particular, the benefits of delaying gratification, rather than going for immediate - and often only perceived - reward, are tangible. When we give our mind control over our emotions in this realm, we feel the results in all areas of our lives.

Student Resource no. 4: **This is Your Brain on Easy Credit**

PowerPoint presentation:

Attitudes to Money

Many financial problems stem from flawed attitudes towards money. So much unnecessary anguish comes from misguided reasoning, which can be remedied with a conscious shift in perspective. Adopting correct, Torah-based attitudes can enable people to manage their finances wisely and avoid countless financial difficulties.

Student Resource no. 5: **Financial Instability: No One is Immune**

C. Establishing Financial Goals

1. The process of achieving financial stability begins with establishing financial goals that reflect your personal values. Once you've established your financial goals, it's time to create a plan for achieving those goals.

2. *Textbook readings:* ***Personal Finance*** Chapter 1, Planning Your Personal Finances, pp. 1-23

- *The Financial Planning Process*, pp. 1-8

  Application: Using the SMART goal-setting guidelines on p. 9, build a realistic set of financial goals for a couple in their first year of marriage.

- *Developing Personal Financial Goals*, pp. 8-11

  Application: Developing Financial Goals exercise, p. 11

- *Influences on Personal Financial Planning*, pp. 11-16

  Application: Using the Rule of 72 (p. 13), calculate how many years it will take to double your money at an interest rate of 5%.

- Opportunity Costs and the Time Value of Money, pp. 16-21.

  Application:

  - Discounting (Present Value):
    Using the time value of money tables in Exhibit 1-8 (p.19) calculate the present value of $1000 received in six years with an interest rate of 5%.
  - Compounding (Future Value):
    Using the time value of money tables in Exhibit 1-8 (p. 19) calculate the future value of $1000 at 6 percent in 10 years.

    - Student Resource no. 6: **Values & Valuables**

  Application: How do you arrange your daily schedule to fit in everything you want to do while maximizing your resources? Remember: Your money is limited. Your physical energy is limited. Your time is limited. All three need to be budgeted carefully so that you can get the most out of your life.

- Achieving Financial Goals, ***Personal Finance*** pp. 21-26

  Application: Using the chart on p. 26 as a model, create a chart that depicts the financial stages and corresponding goals for a typical family in your community. Include columns for 1-year goals, 5-year goals, 10-year goals, and 20-year goals.

Unit 2

Income

Goals:

- To identify considerations in choosing a career
- To optimize career education and training
- To highlight the benefits and drawbacks of entrepreneurship
- To learn how to write a résumé
- To distinguish between hard and soft skills and establish the importance of both
- To understand and apply the concept of scarcity
- To discuss the working woman's reality
- To explore the dynamics of earning a raise
- To learn how to face changing work conditions

A. Self-awareness: What Am I Good At?

1. Choosing a Direction

- Student Resource no. 7: **Chovot Halevavot**

Every person has an innate affinity or interest in a particular vocation or type of commerce and that is the set of tools Hashem gave him to contribute to the world and to earn his living.

2. Explanation

Every person has a unique mission, and is charged by Hashem to make a particular contribution to the world. In order to carry out this mission and contribute that which only he can contribute, a person is given a unique set of tools - things like innate talents, personality, mental prowess, and physical capabilities and stamina.

You should try to ensure that the work you do is suited to your unique strengths, characteristics, and passions. On a spiritual level, this will allow you to maximize your contribution to the world and experience the fulfillment of carrying out the mission with which your soul was charged. On a practical level, it will allow you to maximize your earning power.

3. Misguided reasons for choosing a career

a) Lucrative: "There's a lot of money in that field." Any field can be lucrative or unprofitable, depending on the person and the circumstances. Indeed, the Talmud (*Sanhedrin* 82a) teaches, "There is no vocation that does not have in it poverty and wealth." The amount of money you earn depends on *siyata d'Shemaya*, Heavenly assiatance, and on your ability to carve a niche in your field - whatever that field may be. Salary potential is obviously a major consideration when evaluating a job or field, but it should not be the only consideration.

b) Popular: "Everyone's doing it." If everyone's doing it, that makes it less scarce and therefore less valuable.

c) Available: "It's the only job available." Taking whatever job is available might make sense, at times, if it can be used as a stepping stone or learning experience, or if the alternative is no job at all. But don't passively accept whatever presents itself; you have to be proactive about your career choices. If opportunities don't present themselves at your doorstep - and they usually don't - you have to pursue or create them.

d) Familiar: "It's the family occupation." If people in your family or community work in a certain field, it might be easier for you to break into that field. And if the field is right for you, that's great. But don't embark on a career solely because other people you know do it and it's the path of least resistance.

e) Convenient: "It's right around the corner." The comfort that comes with a convenient job can very quickly morph into boredom and tediousness after you do the job for a while. Better do something inconvenient that makes the most of your talents and abilities than work at a dead-end job that is convenient. If you enjoy what you do, you'll find a way to make it work no matter how inconvenient it is.

4. The right career for you

You choose a career by finding the best fit between your innate abilities and the demands of the economic market. Put differently, we might say that the right career for you is the intersection between what you can uniquely offer and what the world needs. When choosing a career, therefore, you need to ask yourself two questions: What are my strengths? And how can I use those strengths to fill a need and generate income?

Textbook readings: ***Personal Finance*** Chapter 2, Financial Aspects of Career Planning, pp. 46-61

› Career Opportunities: Now and in the Future

Application: Identify a particular career that has changed significantly in the past 20 years - due to social influences, industry trends, and economic conditions - and project how this career will change in the next 20 years.

Employment Search Strategies

Application: Compose a three-minute "elevator speech" describing your experience and skills in a particular area.

Financial and Legal Aspects of Employment

Application: "A better benefits package is worth more than a higher salary." Discuss this statement, giving examples of situations in which it applies and situations in which it does not apply.

Long-Term Career Development

Application: How can a mentor help you at each of the following career stages?

a) Choosing a career.
b) Finding your first job.
c) Weathering the vicissitudes of the employment market.
d) Segueing from your starting job to a more senior position.

B. Education

The right education - both initially and on an ongoing basis - is critical to success in any field. From both a Torah and a practical perspective, however, it makes sense to pursue formal education and career training only to the extent that you need it for your career.

- Student Resource no. 8: **Making Educated Decisions About Education**

Application:

1. List ten careers that require significant post-high-school education and ten careers that require minimal post-high-school education.
2. Of the careers you listed, which are primarily dependent on inborn skill? Which are primarily dependent on skill that is acquired through training or experience?
3. Rank the careers you listed in Question 1 according to the expected income of a person in each of these fields.

C. Entrepreneurship

- Student Resource no. 9: **The Benefits of Entrepreneurship**

1. Benefits

There are three primary ways to earn money: through investments; through working for someone else; and through running your own business. Being your own boss involves responsibility and risk, but it also brings with it lots of potential advantages. When you work for someone else, you are limited to time-based salary or wages, which may not reflect the actual value of the work you are providing. When you work for yourself, however, you have more flexibility and autonomy, as well as greater opportunity to profit.

2. Drawbacks

a) Often requires significant initial investment of money

b) No natural time boundaries - business is not a 9-5 job

c) High risk of failure

(1) Statistics from the U.S. Small Business Administration show that two-thirds of new businesses survive at least two years and forty-four percent survive at least four years. (The previous, long-held belief was that fifty percent of businesses fail in the first year and ninety-five percent fail within five years.) In other words, one out of every two businesses closes within four years.

(2) These statistics are not meant to discourage you, but to help you understand that success in business requires a great deal of hard work and *siyata d'Shemaya*.

3. Do you have the makings of an entrepreneur?

Not everyone is cut out to run a business. Ask yourself these questions:

- Are you an ambitious, self-motivated person? It takes a great deal of discipline, motivation and drive to be your own boss.
- Are you willing to take calculated risks?
- Can you handle the many technicalities that a business entails? To operate a successful business, you need not only vision and imagination, but attention to detail as well.

- Are you flexible enough to constantly adapt your business to changing market conditions, keep up with technological advances and continually refresh your professional abilities?
- Do you have the persistence necessary to steer your business venture through relentless adversity? The stress of getting a business off the ground and keeping it operational often takes a toll on people's physical and emotional health, and can adversely affect their family lives.
- Can you get along with difficult people - a demanding client, for instance?
- Are you good with numbers? Running a business involves plenty of mathematics and number crunching.
- Do you possess good planning and organizational skills?
- Are you an optimistic person?

Some of the skills listed above can be delegated to employees or outsourced, but you'll need to have most of the qualities and a good part of the skills in your own repertoire.

If you answered "yes" to most of the above questions, you have the makings of a good business owner.

Application: Assessing Businesses in Your Community

Which businesses are you familiar with that succeeded? Which businesses are you familiar with that failed? List the factors that led to their success or failure. For instance:

a) Business concept: Did the business fill a real niche?

b) Market research: Did the business owner adjust his business concept to the demands of the market?

c) Business plan: Did the business owner prepare a realistic plan for creating a viable business?

d) Professional business consulting: Did the business owner take professional advice in setting up his business?

e) Breakeven point: Did the business owner calculate how much business he had to do in order to cover his initial expenses and begin profiting?

f) Marketing & advertising: Did people know how to find this business when they needed it?

g) Location: Was the business situated correctly?

Group assignment: Creating a Business Plan - "If you fail to plan, you plan to fail."

Your group will follow the 11 steps outlined in this assignment to develop a basic business plan that will address a demand in your community.

D. Creating Your Résumé

a) What's a résumé or CV, curriculum vitae? A statement of your employment objective along with your academic history and work experience.

b) Why is a résumé important? Your résumé is your introduction to a prospective employer, and it determines what the employer's first impression of you will be. Your résumé is your opportunity to sell yourself, so it has to highlight your skills, talents and strengths, emphasizing the ones most relevant to the position you are trying to get.

c) How to write a good résumé -

- Student Resource no. 10: **How to Write a Good Résumé**

Textbook readings: ***Personal Finance***

Appendix 2 - Résumés, Cover Letters, and Interviews, pp. 67-73

- Developing a Résumé
- Creating a Cover Letter

Application: Following the guidelines in Student Resource 10, write your own résumé and cover letter, for a job objective of your choice. Based on the textbook readings, decide whether to use a chronological, functional, or targeted résumé.

- The Job Interview

Application: Choose a partner, and role-play a job interview, based on the questions on page 74 of the college textbook. Then switch roles.

E. Hard & Soft Skills

- Student Resource no. 11: **Transcending Mediocrity – The Power of Soft Skills**

a) Hard skills: The necessary knowledge and professional ability you need in order to succeed in a particular profession.

b) Soft skills: All the qualities other than knowledge and industry-specific ability that contribute to a person's professional success.

c) Understanding the importance of soft skills: There's a lot more to succeeding in your field than knowledge and know-how. Many people have excellent hard skills, yet remain mediocre in terms of both their earnings and upward mobility. Generally, it's soft skills that make the difference between a mediocre worker and an excellent one.

d) Three categories of soft skills:

1) Business skills (e.g., networking, teamwork ability, conscientiousness, negotiation)

2) People skills (e.g., empathy, listening, communication)

3) Personal skills (e.g., reliability, integrity, cheerfulness, humility)

Application:

1. How can a starting job-seeker use soft skills to compensate for lack of hard skills or experience? Give a specific example.
2. What are some skills you have that you feel you can draw on when applying for a job?

Note: This is an excellent vehicle for getting students to focus on their unique and often unsung strengths.

F. Scarcity

- Student Resource no. 12: **The Scarcity Principle**

How much you are paid for the work that you do is determined by the laws of supply and demand. The scarcer your skills or services are in relation to the demand for those skills or services, the more you can earn.

Application: Think of someone you know who has successfully carved out a niche in a particular field. Using the "scarcity principle," analyze why this person has met with success.

G. Earning a Raise - Every Day at Work

1) Justifications for asking for a raise:

   a) Inflation pushes the cost of living up continually, and your salary should go up continually to reflect that.

   b) You become more and more valuable to your company the longer you work for them, and you should be paid more for the additional experience you bring to the job each year.

   c) If your job description has broadened to include new responsibilities, if your skills have improved, or if your performance has exceeded expectations, then you are now worth more as an employee than you were when you were hired, and you should be compensated accordingly.

2) How to get a raise

   a) Earn the raise

   b) Ask for it.

Asking for a raise is not something you will do very often, but earning a raise is something you should be doing during every moment that you are at work. Your employer has to believe that your salary is money well spent, and you therefore have to prove to her that your value as an employee more than justifies the cost to the company. To do that, you need to continually increase your value as an employee. How do you accomplish this? By taking the initiative to acquire new skills. By showing willingness to assume additional responsibilities. By pinch-hitting for your colleagues and taking up the slack. By going the extra mile when necessary and making yourself available when you are needed. And by demonstrating, through action and attitude, that you care about the company.

Application: Give several possible reasons that people might be reluctant to ask for a raise. Which of these reasons are valid? Which of them are unnecessarily paralyzing? What advice would you give a reluctant but deserving employee to overcome these obstacles?

H. Facing Changing Work Conditions

Plotting a successful career path involves careful advance planning and constant maneuvering. It's important to understand the various conditions that can put a damper on - or an end to - your career. Identifying these conditions will allow you to navigate your career journey successfully and steadily enhance your income.

1) Weathering down times: A down time at work can be caused by any challenge that isn't allowing you to earn as much as you could be earning or as much as others in your field are earning. Generally, it's a sign that you have to improve your skills (hard or soft), work harder, become more efficient, or even move to a different company. But you don't have to - and you shouldn't - abandon the type of work you're doing just because you're experiencing a dip.

2) Hitting a brick wall: This happens when you've reached the maximum salary potential for the type of work you're doing and you no longer have the possibility of upward mobility. In other words, there's no good reason why someone should pay you more for the work you're able to do. If you are at a dead end, and you decide that you need to earn more and advance your career, it is time for a significant career shift.

3) Anticipating when your career is about to come to an abrupt end: In today's economy, jobs are constantly being automated or outsourced. Many careers that existed a few years ago no longer exist today, and many careers that exist today will no longer exist in a few years.

- Student Resource no. 13: **Beware! Changing Road Conditions Ahead**

    Application: Identify five fields that have become obsolete in the past 20 years, and use your imagination to think of five fields that will be created or will move to center stage in the next twenty years.

I. The Working Woman's Reality

Note: The issue of woman's role - career vs. home - is a very hot topic. Allow for guided discussion that will enable students to reach correct conclusions on their own.

1. Career considerations

    a) Time: How many hours a day are you willing to devote to earning income?

b) Earning power: How much money will you make at a particular job?

c) Responsibility: What level of work responsibility and stress are you willing to shoulder? Do you want a job that you can walk away from or one that you take home with you?

d) Ambition: "Working woman" vs. "career woman."

2. Workplace environment

3. Family responsibilities

4. Ambition vs. Loyalty to your employer

Application: Reflect upon the opportunity costs involved in each of the following career options for a young mother:

- Full-time mom
- Stay-at-home mom with minimal side income
- Part-time job, part-time homemaker
- Nine-to-five, low-stress job
- Full-time-plus career

J. Working from Home

1. Advantages

a) Time flexibility

b) Family availability

c) Financial savings: transportation, wardrobe, office space, home office tax deductions

2. Disadvantages

a) Distractions

b) Social isolation

c) No demarcation between professional and personal life

- Student Resource no. 14: **Working From Home, and Making It Work!**

Application: The merits of employees working at home versus working in the office have generated intense debate among corporate management. If you were managing a company, would you prefer to have your employees working from home or working in the office? Why?

K. Taxes

PowerPoint presentation:
Taxes

PowerPoint Review Questions:

1. How is net income calculated?
2. List five different kinds of taxes, and identify whether they are federal, state, or city taxes.
3. What are the steps in creating a new tax and drafting it into law?
4. Contrast Form 1040 and Form W-2, explaining who would use each one.

Textbook readings: ***Personal Finance*** Chapter 4, Planning Your Tax Strategy, pp. 106-121

- Taxes and Financial Planning
- Income Tax Fundamentals

Application: Different U.S. states have different levels of taxation (see side note on p. 106, in *Personal Finance*). Discuss the pros and cons of living in a "tax-friendly" state such as Delaware, and living in a state with high taxation, such as New York.

Application: Explain the following terms: earned income, passive income, capital gains, exclusion, tax credit, tax shelter, tax deduction, audit, tax evasion

Unit 3

Budgeting

Goals:

- To understand what a budget is and why it's necessary to have one
- To examine the step-by-step process of building and following a budget
- To explain the concept of cash flow and learn how to build a cash flow plan
- To learn how to keep finances orderly by distinguishing between the various aspects of one's finances
- To understand basic banking and checking procedures

Note: *This unit is designed to be studied in conjunction with the Mesila Student Guide to Budgeting that appears as unit three in the Student Text and unit four in this one. The following is an overview,with references to the appropriate pages in the Mesila Student Guide to Budgeting.*

1. What's a Budget?

Budgeting means managing any type of limited resource. In this case it's a plan for managing your money, based on your estimated income and expenses.

The idea of budgeting one's money makes many people tense, because they automatically associate "budget" with "I cannot afford what I want." A creative and effective way of introducing this topic is to discuss and/or have a class exercise in budgeting time or some other resource - i.e., "You have 3 hours available and you have the following tasks you'd like to accomplish. How will you budget your time? What will you give up? What is indispensable?" This exercise will lay the foundations for the principles of budgeting, which can then be easily transferred to financial budgeting.

2. Why Budget?

(see Part 4 - Mesila Guide to Budgeting, p. 4)

a. Control over your finances

b. Freedom to decide what you want to do with your money

c. Reduced financial stress

3. First Step: Prioritize

(see Part 4 - Mesila Guide to Budgeting, p. 5-7)

a. Our goal in budgeting is to allow you to have everything you need and some of what you want. That means that you have to know the difference between what you need and what you want.

   Note: This is a good place for class discussion about how to distinguish needs from wants, how it will differ in different societies, etc.

b. Needs before wants: Make sure you are aware of what your needs are so that you can fit them into your budget first, and only then see which of your wants can fit in.

c. Urgent vs. non-urgent: Discussion - what's the difference between urgent and important? When does the urgent override the important and vice versa?

d. Types of expenses:

   1) Fixed monthly expenses: mortgage or rent, insurance (life, health, home, auto, etc.), car payments, childcare, savings plans, domestic help, etc.
   2) Fluctuating monthly expenses: food, utilities (telephone, cellular phone, electricity, water, gas, etc.), gasoline, etc.
   3) Annual/Periodic expenses: summer camp, medical and dental costs, vacations and outings, home repairs

e. Tracking your expenses

   1) Why track? Knowing what you spend your money on and how much you spend will put you more in control of your money and help you make smarter spending decisions. Knowledge is power.

   2) How to track expenses: See addendum - The Mesila Guide to Budgeting

   3) Exercise: Track What You Spend!
   For one week, track every single expense, even a can of soda, as well as every bit of income, including allowance, tutoring, babysitting. The goal is not yet to balance expenses and income, but to raise awareness.

4. Building a Family Budget

(see Part 4 - Mesila Guide to Budgeting, p. 8-15 & 35)

a. Monthly vs. Annual Budgeting

   1) Some expenses occur every month, while others crop up once a year or periodically.

   2) One of the most common mistakes people make in budgeting is calculating

their monthly expenses but failing to take annual/periodic expenses into account. This is often the reason why people find themselves "not making it" when on paper their income seems adequate for their expenses.

3) Cash

4) Checks

5) Credit cards

6) Debit cards

b. Cash Flow Planning

1) Definition: Cash flow planning means ensuring that you have the money you need when you need it

2) Why is cash flow planning necessary? Income and expenses are not static - they fluctuate over the year. In order to ride out these peaks and troughs, you need to plan your budget to accommodate your cash flow needs.

c. Support material: Mesila budgeting forms

5. Maintaining Order: The Divide-and-Conquer Approach

(see Part 4 - Mesila Guide to Budgeting, p. 26-31)

a. Distinguishing between the many aspects of your finances is important because:

1) It helps you to gain an awareness of exactly what is happening with your money.

2) It puts you in control of your finances by enabling you to make informed decisions.

b. Differentiate between:

1) short-term and long-term expenses (e.g., weddings and retirement)

2) small purchases and major costs

3) predictable expenses and emergency/unforeseen expenses

4) personal expenses and business expenses

5) income and assets

6) ongoing expenses and debt

6. How Do I Know If My Budget Is Workable?

(see Part 4 - Mesila Guide to Budgeting, p. 32-34)

a. A good budget is one that does all of the following:

1) Generously covers all essentials

2) Leaves some room for non-essentials
3) Makes provisions for unanticipated expenses
4) Incorporates both short- and long-term savings

b. A budget has to be tested and adjusted, and updated regularly.

7. Long-term budget

(see Part 4 - Mesila Guide to Budgeting, p. 16-19)

a) Covers major expenses anticipated during the next few years
b) Includes both expected and unexpected expenses
c) Includes realistic savings and debt repayment strategies

8. Basic Banking and Checking Procedures

PowerPoint presentation:

Basic banking and checking procedures

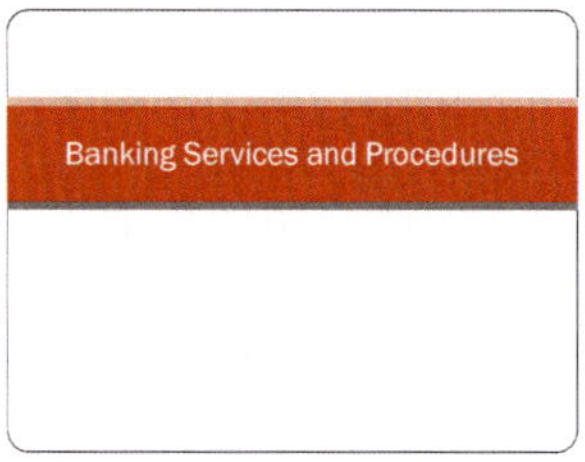

PowerPoint Review Questions:

1. List the different types of bank accounts.
2. What steps can you take to minimize check fraud?
3. Why is it important to keep your checkbook balanced?

Textbook readings: ***Personal Finance*** Chapter 3, Money Management Strategy: Financial Statements and Budgeting, pp. 77-96

Application: "LIFE is a major budget buster" (page 92). "LIFE," in this context, is an acronym for: Listed, Impulse buying, Forgotten, and Emergencies. Explain.

Application: On page 93, there is a table of typical budget allocation, in percentages. Create a similar table for typical budget allocations of families in your community.

Application: Using the chart on page 96, compare and contrast the different budgeting systems.

Unit 4

Savings and Investments

Goals:

- To understand the importance of savings
- To understand the various types of insurance and how they work
- To examine different investment options
- To explain the risk/return equation
- To discover the power of compound interest

Note: Many students are just entering the world of employment and may be intoxicated by the idea of having their own money to spend. Before getting into the details of how to save and/or invest, initiate class discussion on the value of calculated saving rather than wanton spending.

Textbook Readings: ***Personal Finance***

pp. 97-98: Identifying Savings Goals, Selecting a Saving Technique, Calculating Savings Amounts

Application: List five possible reasons for savings.

pp. 150-158: Savings Plans, Evaluating Savings Plans

Application: Evaluate the pros and cons of each the following options:

1. A regular savings account versus a certificate of deposit (CD)
2. A money-market account versus a money-market fund
3. A three-month certificate of deposit versus a one-year certificate of deposit

A. Savings

Savings are a loan to yourself. It is no harder to put money away beforehand than to repay money afterward - you will need to strain yourself either way. The question is: Whom are you paying? If you save, you end up paying yourself. (And you pay less money, because it's without interest, and also without embarrassment.) If you borrow, you are left with nothing at the end. And you have the stress of being beholden to someone and their repayment terms.

- **Torah view of savings**

> כל מי שיש לו פת בסלו ואומר מה אוכל למחר אינו אלא מקטני אמנה.
> *One who has bread in his basket and says, "What will I eat tomorrow?" has a minimum of belief. (Sotah 48b)*

- **Discussion:**

  How do we reconcile that concept with planning for the future?

B. Insurance

1. Insurance & Risk Management

Textbook Readings: ***Personal Finance*** Chapter 10, pp. 317-320

Application: Define the following terms:

Policy, premium, rider, deductible, claim, appraisal, annuity, liability, third-party liability

2. Property & Liability Insurance

Textbook Readings: ***Personal Finance*** pp. 322-332

Application:

a. What is the difference between property and liability insurance, and why are they both important for a homeowner?
b. What are the main types of coverage included in home insurance policies?
c. Explain the two methods insurance companies use to settle claims (actual cash value and replacement value).

3. Automobile Insurance

Textbook Readings: ***Personal Finance*** pp. 332-340

Application:

a. What does "driver classification" mean?
b. What factors are used to determine driver classification?
c. Discuss three ways to reduce driver insurance premiums.

4. Life Insurance

Textbook Readings: **Personal Finance** Chapter 12, pp. 388-395

Application: What are the four ways to assess your life insurance needs?

- Student Resource no. 15: **Life Insurance - To Buy or Not to Buy?**

  Review Questions: Why might someone believe that life insurance is problematic according to Jewish law or tradition? Why is this belief mistaken?

- The Maharsha states in his *Chiddushei Aggadot* (*Niddah* 65b) that a person should put aside money for his old age.
- In his Responsa *Shevet Halevi* (4:1), Harav Shmuel Wosner *shlit"a* writes, "It is obvious that [for] something that is the nature of the world, such as old age or marrying off children... it is a mitzvah to prepare in advance so that he will not become dependent on others."

C. Investments

1. Definition

Making your money work for you in order to make you more money.

Textbook Readings: **Personal Finance** Preparing for an Investment Program, pp. 424-430

Application: Why is it important to make sure your finances are stable before deciding to invest?

Application: Explain the benefits of beginning to invest at a young age, even with a small amount of money.

2. Types of Investments

a) **Bank investments**

- The infinitesimal risks associated with bank investments make these the safest investments available. Because the risks are so low, the returns are also very low, occasionally lower than the rate of inflation. Bank investments are suitable for people with no risk tolerance, or for people who require immediate liquidity.
- Types of bank investments:

  (1) Savings account: an account in a bank on which interest is paid

  (2) Money market fund: a mutual fund which invests in short-term financial instruments, such as treasury bills and commercial paper

b) **Securities: Stocks & Bonds**

- Stock: the capital invested in a company or corporation through the buying of shares, each of which entitles the buyer to a share in the ownership and, usually, dividends, voting rights, etc.
- Bond: an interest-bearing certificate issued by a government or business, promising to pay the holder a specified sum on a specified date: it is a common means of raising capital funds
- Mutual fund: a fund consisting of a number of diversified securities that is owned jointly by those who have purchased shares in it as an investment
- Hedge fund: a partnership of investors who pool large sums for trading in securities, often taking large risks, as by buying with borrowed funds or selling short

Textbook Readings: ***Personal Finance*** Chapter 14, Investing in Stocks, pp. 460-487

Application: Why do corporations issue common stock? Why do investors buy these stocks?

Application: Compare and contrast the techniques appropriate for long-term and short-term stock investments.

Textbook Readings: ***Personal Finance*** Chapter 15, Investing in Bonds, pp. 499-526

Application: Bonds have traditionally been considered a safer investment than stocks. Why?

Application: Why would a corporation sell bonds? Give five possible reasons.

Textbook Readings: ***Personal Finance*** Chapter 16, Investing in Mutual Funds, pp. 536-561

Application: Explain, as you would to a novice investor, the steps in choosing and purchasing mutual funds.

Application: What are two major reasons that people invest in mutual funds?

Application: List the pros and cons of investing in mutual funds.

c) **Real estate**

Residential Real Estate

There are two types of potential earnings from residential real estate investments:

(a) Rent

(b) Capital gains (in the form of rising property value): The amount by which the selling price of an asset exceeds the purchase price; the gain is realized when the asset is sold.

(Definitions of above terms taken from Webster's New World Dictionary)

Textbook Readings: ***Personal Finance*** Chapter 17, Investing in Real Estate and Other Investment Alternatives, pp. 570-580

Application: Explain this statement: Your home is a hedge against inflation.

Application: Give a brief description of the following types of real estate investments: commercial property, undeveloped land, foreclosures.

Application: Discuss four advantages and four disadvantages of investing in real estate.

Note: Bring in sample ads offering seemingly attracive real-estate deals in farflung locations and discuss the dangers of bogus real-estate sales.

PowerPoint presentation:

Savings & Investments

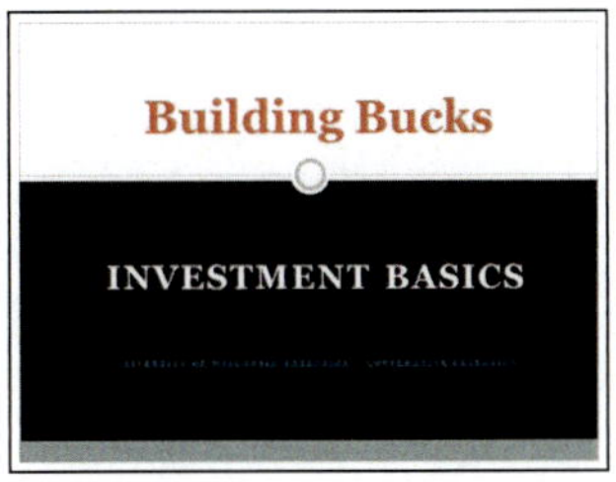

Review Questions:

1. Explain the difference between saving and investing.
2. On what basis should you choose a financial advisor?
3. What are warning signs of fraudulent investments?

Textbook Readings: ***Personal Finance*** Chapter 13, Investing Fundamentals Preparing for an Investment Program, pp. 424-429

Application: "Regardless of the reason, the creation of wealth is a worthy goal" (textbook, p. 424). How is this statement at odds with Torah outlook?

D. Matching Your Savings Needs to Your Investment Strategies

1. The Risk/Return Equation

Investing, by definition, means risking capital for the sake of an anticipated future gain, or return. As a rule, return is directly proportional to risk - the greater the risk, the higher the potential return. The converse is true as well: the higher the potential return, the greater the risk.

Textbook Readings: ***Personal Finance*** Factors Affecting the Choice of Investments, Asset Allocation and Investment Alternatives, pp. 430-444

Application: Using the chart on p. 431, list the factors that go into assessing a person's tolerance for risk.

Textbook Readings: ***Personal Finance*** Factors that Reduce Investment Risk, pp. 444-446

Application: How do each of the following reduce your investment risk?

a. Careful evaluation of investments and due diligence

b. Continual monitoring of your investments

c. Keeping orderly records of your investments

- Student Resource no. 16: **Making Millions on Dinars**

  Young couples often have a nest egg that they are eager to invest. There are a lot of investments out there that promise sky-high returns - and carry with them sky-high risks. Currency speculation is one of them.

- Student Resource no. 17: **The Myth of Guaranteed Returns**

  If an investment is offering more interest than the bank offers, that means the bank is afraid to invest (otherwise they'd get financing from the bank). Is your risk appetite greater than the bank's?

2. Short-Term vs. Long-Term Savings

- Short-term savings: The money you'll need for emergencies and for foreseeable large expenses.
- Long-term savings: The money you'll need for times of considerable financial strain, such as marrying off children and old age.

• Student Resource no. 18: **Savings: The Long & Short of It**

Your short-term savings goals and long-term savings goals require different strategies.

3. Liquidity

Being in cash or easily convertible to cash. This is an important consideration when saving or investing your money - how quickly and easily can it be converted to cash?

4. Tax Shelters

A way of investing money to reduce the taxes incurred on current earnings.

5. Types of Interest

› **Interest**

a) Simple interest: interest calculated on principal alone, and not on principal plus interest (this is rarely relevant in investments or borrowing)

b) Compound interest: interest calculated on the sum of the principal and the accrued interest (this is the type of interest typically earned on investments and paid on loans or credit cards)

c) The power of compound interest: Over time, compound interest causes the principal to grow exponentially.

• Student Resource no. 19: **The Time Value of Money**

The time value of money is the increase in an amount of money due to interest earned. Investing money rather than spending it today gives you a future amount worth more than you have now.

Textbook Readings: ***Personal Finance*** Chapter 13, p. 430, Using the Time Value of Money to Calculate Investment Returns

Review Questions: Using the table on p. 430, calculate:

(a) Each year on Rachel's birthday, her grandmother puts $1000 in a money market account fund that accrues 2%. After ten years, how much would her investment be worth? How much would it have been worth had she not invested it?

(b) Had Rachel's money been invested in an investment that paid 6%, how much would her investment have been worth after ten years?

- Student Resource no. 20: **Sample Heter Iska Form for Business Loans**

Heter Iska: An agreement made between a borrower and a lender transforming a loan into an investment and turning borrower and lender into investor and manager who share in the possible profits or losses.

Unit 5

Spending and Credit

Goals:

- To examine the various methods of payment and learn how to use each one optimally
- To examine the positive and negative aspects of consumerism
- To understand the importance of credit and how to build a good credit history
- To illustrate the advantages and pitfalls of credit cards

A. Payment Methods - Pros and Cons

- Student Resource no. 21: **Payment Methods chart**

Textbook Readings: ***Personal Finance*** Chapter 5, Payment Methods, pp. 158-164

- Electronic Payments

Application: "Transactions not involving cash, checks, or credit cards have expanded with technology, improved security, and increased consumer acceptance" (p. 158). Explain how the three factors listed (technology, improved security, and increased consumer acceptance) have promoted the popularity of electronic payments.

Reflection: In your opinion, is the trend toward electronic payments a positive or a negative development?

- Types of Checking Accounts, Evaluating Checking Accounts, Managing Your Checking Accounts

Application: See p. 162, "Reconciling Your Checking Account": Why is it important to keep your checkbook register up to date? What are the potential hazards of neglecting to reconcile your checkbook?

B. Consumerism

1. Consumerism: Great for the Economy

a. Consumerism - definition: The theory that increasing consumption is economically beneficial

b. Increased consumption and spending leads to higher standard of living, improved quality of life and greater national wealth.

c. In other words: Shopping, buying, owning, acquiring are great for the economy, and therefore have been actively encouraged in the past century.

d. A healthy economy is dependent upon the movement of currency. When you buy groceries, the grocery owner can pay his tuition, and then the teachers and principals can buy food in the grocery. It's a cycle - money moves from hand to hand, benefiting everyone. When money doesn't move, and people don't spend, that results in a recession or depression.

e. This concept is supported in Torah sources as well:

> ולמה נקרא שמם זוזין? שזזים מזה ונותנין לזה
>
> *Why is [money] called "zuzin"? Because it moves ["zaz"] from one and is given to another.* (Bamidbar Rabbah 22:7)

f. Because spending has the power to create prosperity, people are encouraged to support local stores and businesses. This, too, is a Torah value:

> נכנסו חכמי ישראל אצלו, אמרו לו: אדונינו המלך, עמך ישראל צריכין פרנסה.
>
> אמר להם: לכו והתפרנסו זה מזה.
>
> *The Sages of Israel came to [Dovid Hamelech] and said to him, "Our master, the king, your nation Israel needs sustenance!" He said to them, "Go and earn a living from one another."* (Berachot 3b)

g. Better than giving charity is giving people money in a dignified way, by employing them or patronizing their businesses.

2. Consumerism: Great for the Economy, But What About for Me?

a. Spending stimulates the economy, but at what cost to the individual?

b. The spending cycle - economically:

1. People are encouraged to spend money to stimulate the economy
2. People spend money, rather than conserve it
3. People start to need more because they have accustomed themselves to more
    - i. People run out of money and don't have savings to dip into
    - ii. People can't afford the things the things they are accustomed to
    - iii. People borrow money in order to pay for what they need and want
4. People fall into debt, which causes financial stress
5. Inability to maintain the standard of living that one has become accustomed to results in stress and reduced quality of life

c. The impact of consumerism on people's values

1. People spend money, at the persuasion of advertising, rather than in response to real need.
2. The more they have, the more they need; consumerism is based on creating needs where none existed before

    Example: "The Lorax" by Dr. Seuss -

    Student Resource no 22: **Dr. Seuss on Consumerism**

3. People become busier with spending
4. Advertising trains people to fill voids with spending
    - i. People busy themselves with things instead of ideas
    - ii. Relationships become shallow
    - iii. Aspirations become materialistic and technical rather than value-based
    - iv. People identify themselves with what they have and how they look rather than with their actions and character
    - v. People fill voids in their life by acquisitions and shopping rather than introspection and growth
    - vi. People are left feeling empty - and then they go spend more

3. Torah View of Consumerism

The Torah view of consumerism: Acquisition is not a value, but rather a tool toward reaching higher goals. Shopping and acquiring possessions is NOT a positive, constructive activity in and of itself, but rather a necessary chore.

4. Discussion: Shopping as Retail Therapy?

Note: Shopping is a favorite pastime for teens and young adults. Shopping malls do their part to transform the shopping trip into an "experience." Open the floor to discussion of the topic and guide the responses towards the desired conclusions.

People often go shopping as a form of leisure or to fill an emotional void. Is shopping a valid form of therapy or recreation? In what ways can this become a detrimental habit?

Student Resource no. 23: **Am I a Shopaholic?**

Supplementary material: Downsize to Upgrade - The Art of Living with Less
(see Mesila Guide to Budgeting, p. 36).

5. Becoming an Informed Consumer

Textbook readings: ***Personal Finance:***

- Chapter 8, Consumer Protection Strategies and Legal Protection
- Financial Implications of Consumer Decisions, Practical Purchasing Strategies, pp. 252-260

Application: What are the opportunity costs of each of the following choices? (Reminder: Opportunity cost means cost in terms of foregoing alternatives - if I buy this, I can't buy that.)

a) Purchasing items on credit

b) Purchasing cheaper, low-quality items

c) Purchasing expensive, high-quality items

d) Purchasing items online

e) Comparison shopping

f) Impulse buying

Application: A sign in an electronics store advertises a computer on sale for $560 or 12 monthly payments of $50. What are the opportunity costs of each payment option?

- Resolving Consumer Complaints

Textbook readings: ***Personal Finance*** pp. 269-276

Application: What are four steps for resolving consumer complaints?

Discussion: Give examples of cases in which each step would be appropriate. Give examples of cases in which certain steps would be inappropriate.

C. Understanding Credit

A. Credit - definition: The ability to pay later for goods or services

B. Credit history - definition: The record of one's past borrowing and repayment patterns, including information about late payments and bankruptcy

C. Why does credit history matter? Because when you apply for any sort of loan, mortgage, credit card, or financing, the lender will check your credit history to see whether you repaid previous commitments and whether you repaid them in a timely manner. If you have a bad credit history, or even if you don't have any credit history, you will have a very hard time convincing a bank or any company to lend you money or issue you a credit card.

D. Credit rating - definition: A score assigned to a person or business based on their credit history by which lenders can assess their likelihood to repay.

E. How do you establish a good credit history and credit rating?

A few tips:

1. By obtaining and using credit
    a. It's important to apply for a credit card and use it in order to start your credit history. 15% of your credit rating is determined by how long you've been borrowing.
    b. As you develop a good credit history, you can slowly apply for an increasingly higher credit limit so that you become a more "credit-worthy" consumer.

c. Although you need to use some of the credit extended to you in order to establish credit history, you should not use a high percentage of your credit limit, because that makes you a credit risk.

d. Too many inquiries into your credit history will damage your credit rating

Note: The purpose of using credit is not to borrow money to pay for purchases you can't afford; it's to establish yourself as a worthy borrower so that you can obtain credit in the future for big-ticket items such as mortgage or auto financing.

2. By making sure to pay your bills on time, whether it's your bill at the dentist or electric bill

3. By paying your credit card statement in full every month, on time, and never missing a minimum payment

Textbook readings: ***Personal Finance***

Chapter 7, The Cost of Credit, pp. 218-228

- Finance Charge and Annual Percentage Rate (APR)
- The Minimum Monthly Payment Trap

Application: Why would credit card companies subtly encourage their clients to make only monthly payments, rather than pay off their full balance each month?

D. Credit Cards: Pros and Cons

1. Advantages

a. Convenient and available
b. Insurance against theft
c. Easy to cancel in the event of loss
d. Payment can be made by telephone or online
e. Can be used anywhere in the world
f. Can be used by all members of the family
g. Easy to track
h. Credit limits make it impossible to spend more than a certain amount.

i. Payment can be made in installments.

j. Earn air miles and rewards

2. Pitfalls

a. Credit cards deceive people into thinking that they have money when they really do not.

b. People spend more because it is convenient and because they do not feel the pain of parting with their money.

c. Multiple credit cards can lead to chaos.

d. Missing a minimum payment can lead interest rates to skyrocket.

e. Carrying a balance from month to month (which over 60% of users do)

f. Sky-high interest rates: The difference between a low interest rate and a high interest rate can be enormous:

Someone with an $8,000 credit card balance who makes minimum monthly payments of 2.5% of the balance:

Amount of Loan	What's the interest rate?	How long will it take to pay off?	How much interest will be paid in total?
$8,000	18%	30 years	$ 11,615.32
$8,000	12%	20 years, 1 month	$ 5,180.13
$8,000	9%	18 years, 2 months	$ 3,334.52
$8,000	5.9%	16 years, 1 month	$ 1,907.18

3. Climbing the Mountain of Credit Card Debt

Supplementary material:

PowerPoint presentation:
The ABCs of Credit Card Finance

- Student Resource no 24: <u>**Climbing the Mountain of Credit Card Debt**</u>

Unit 6

Loans & Borrowing

Goals:

- To differentiate between the various types of loans
- To introduce the benefits and costs of home ownership
- To discuss the positive and negative aspects of loans from religious and practical viewpoints
- To understand the psychological aspects of borrowing
- To examine strategies for debt management

Note: Open with discussion of loans - good or bad? Steer discussion towards recognition that loans can be dangerous when not controlled but may be necessary at times. Important to benefit from loans with great caution.

A. Types of Loans

1. Bank loan
2. Line of credit
3. Business loan
4. Student loan
5. Gemach loans
6. Private loans
   a. From friends or family
   b. From finance companies or private commercial lenders
7. Store credit

Textbook readings: ***Personal Finance***
Sources of Consumer Credit, pp. 213-218

Application: What questions should people ask themselves before taking a loan? Note: In addition to the questions posed by the textbook, one also needs to consider the halachic permissibility of doing so and the hashkafic issues involved, as explained below.

Application: What are the pros and cons of loans from the following sources?

B. Mortgages

1. ***In-Class Exercise:*** Mortgage Payments & Interest -

- Student Resource no. 25: **Mortgage Payments & Interest**

2 Hidden benefits of home ownership

   a. Property values typically rise over time.

   b. Rents go up because of inflation; mortgages don't. That means that even if paying a mortgage is difficult at first, it usually becomes easier as time goes on.

   c. You have equity (value of the property minus the amount owed on it), which offers a measure of financial stability.

   d. Psychological comfort of owning your own home and feeling settled

3. Hidden costs of home ownership

   a. Property tax

   b. Utilities

   c. Maintenance (more cleaning, gardening, home upkeep, extermination, etc.)

   d. Transportation costs are higher when you live in the periphery

   e. Tuition goes up when you are a homeowner

   f. Homeowner's insurance

Textbook readings: ***Personal Finance***

- Housing Alternatives, pp. 282-284

Application: What are some factors to consider when deciding where to live and what type of residence to live in? For a Torah-observant family, what additional factors would need to be considered?

- Renting vs. Buying, pp. 284-286

Application: Using the chart on page 285, list four common housing options and give an example of the type of people who would be suited to each one.

- Renting Your Residence, pp. 286-291

Application: Generally, families begin by renting an apartment or house before purchasing their own house. Why is this a good idea?

- The Home-Buying Process, pp. 291-298

Application:

1. List the benefits and drawbacks of home ownership.
2. What is the purpose of a home inspection?
3. Buying a more spacious home comes at a cost. Why might people decide to purchase a home that is larger than their family currently needs? Why might they decide to buy a home that is just adequate for their current housing needs?

- The Finances of Home Buying, pp. 298-308

Application:

1. On what basis is a person's eligibility for a mortgage determined?
2. What is the correlation between interest rates and the type of home a person can afford?
3. What are typical sources of funding for a down payment?
4. What hidden costs are involved in home purchasing?
5. In what cases would refinancing a mortgage be appropriate?
6. Home ownership scenarios: Contrast the approaches taken by the two couples above. What are the long-term ramifications of each approach?

Couple #1	**Couple #2**
Samuel and Sarah Refael have an $80,000 nest egg: $60,000 put away from wedding money and money that Suri has been saving since high school, plus $20,000 that their parents gave them toward a house, which costs them $285,000. They take out a $205,000 mortgage, and they scrimp and save to meet their $1400 mortgage payments, which is slightly more than they can afford. To ensure that they can meet their payments, they cut a lot of corners: they don't take vacations, they manage with an old car, they don't buy take-out or extras in the supermarket, and they buy clothing only at end-of-season sales. Within five years, the value of their house climbs to $380,000.	Avi and Ayala Sutton have $80,000 from an insurance settlement that Avi received after being in a car accident. They put the money into a savings account and dip into it as needed - for furniture, a car, little gifts for each other and for their friends, going out to eat. They are renting a house for $1400/month, which is slightly more than they can afford, but when the going gets tough, they always have their nest egg to fall back on. Within five years, the $80,000 is gone - and their rent has gone up to $1700.

C. Loan Guarantees (ערבות)

1. Loan guarantee - definition: A promise by one party (the guarantor) to assume the debt obligation of a borrower if that borrower defaults on the loan.
2. Often, receiving a loan is dependent upon procuring guarantors who will agree to pay back the loan in the event that the borrower defaults.
3. Giving a loan guarantee is essentially equivalent to giving a loan, because you are enabling the person to borrow.
4. Giving a guarantee is also essentially equivalent to taking a loan, because you may be called upon - and required - to repay the loan if the borrower defaults (which is always a possibility).
5. You cannot sign a loan guarantee unless you are capable of repaying the other person's loan - and willing to do so.

D. Torah View of Loans

1. Torah commandment to lend money: אִם כֶּסֶף תַּלְוֶה אֶת עַמִּי - When you will lend my nation money (Shemot 22:24) - see Unit VII, charity section. But what about taking a loan? That's not a mitzvah. In fact, let's see what the Torah's view on taking loans is:
2. Loans are inherently negative and problematic
   a. In Birkat Hamazon, we say -

      ונא אל תצריכנו לא לידי מתנת בשר ודם ולא לידי הלוואתם

      Please do not make us needy of the gifts of human hands nor of their loans.

      This shows that taking loans is something inherently negative.

   b. Loans are a curse:
      1. In the blessings of Parashat Ki Tavo:

      "יִפְתַּח ה' לְךָ אֶת אוֹצָרוֹ הַטּוֹב אֶת הַשָּׁמַיִם לָתֵת מְטַר אַרְצְךָ בְּעִתּוֹ וּלְבָרֵךְ אֵת כָּל מַעֲשֵׂה יָדֶךָ וְהִלְוִיתָ גּוֹיִם רַבִּים וְאַתָּה לֹא תִלְוֶה".

      Hashem will open for you His treasure-house of goodness, the heavens, to give the rain of your loand in its time and to bless all your handiwork and you will lend to many nations and you will not borrow". (Devarim 28:12)

2. In the curses of Parashat Ki Tavo (*Devarim* 28:44):

> הוּא יַלְוְךָ וְאַתָּה לֹא תַלְוֶנּוּ.
>
> *He will lend to you and you will not lend to him.*

c. *Kovetz Igrot* of *Chazon Ish*, 2nd volume:

> ...לשלוח יד בהלוואות, המשחית את אצילות הנפש, וגורם בושה לעצמך ולאחרים.
>
> *...To extend your hand for loans, which destroy the soul's nobility, and cause shame to yourself and to others.*

3. If a loan comes with interest it's even worse (even if it's halachically permissible).

4. The word for "interest" in the Torah is נשך, from the root word "to bite"

> **נשך** - רבית שהוא כנשיכת נחש שנושך חבורה קטנה ברגלו ואינו מרגיש ופתאום הוא מבצבץ ונופח עד קדקדו כך רבית אינו מרגיש ואינו ניכר עד שהרבית עולה ומחסרו ממון הרבה.
>
> *Interest - which the Torah calls neshech, similar to the Hebrew word for "bite," neshichah - is like a snakebite. When a snake bites, it creates a small wound in a person's leg, which he does not sense, but suddenly, it puffs up and swells until his head. Similarly, a person does not notice interest until it grows and costs him a great deal of money.* (Shemot Rabbah 31:6)

5. Loans are not just hashkafically problematic, they may also be halachically forbidden at times:

a. One who borrows and does not repay is called a rasha - wicked.

> ארבעה נקראו רשעים... והלווה ואינו משלם שנאמר (תהלים לז) לוה רשע ולא ישלם וצדיק חונן ונותן.
>
> *Four people are called "evildoers"...and one who borrows and does not repay, as it says (Tehillim 37), An evildoer borrows and does not repay, while a righteous person is gracious and gives.* (Bamidbar Rabbah 18:12)

b. One should not lend money to someone who will be unable to repay unless he is willing to write off the loan as charity.

אסור ללוה לקחת הלואה ולהוציאה שלא לצורך ולאבדה עד שלא ימצא המלוה ממה לגבות חובו ואם עושה כן נקרא רשע וכשהמלוה מכיר את הלוה שהוא בעל מדה זו מוטב שלא להלוותו ממה שילווהו ויצטרך לנגשו אחר כך ויעבור בכל פעם משום לא תהיה לו כנושה:

A borrower is forbidden to take a loan and spend it unnecessarily and squander it to the point where the lender cannot collect his due. If he does this, he is called an evildoer, and if the lender knows that the borrower possesses this tendency [of squandering borrowed money], it is preferable not to lend him money rather than lend him and then have to pressure him later, each time violating the prohibition of, "You shall not act as a creditor to him.

c. You may not take a loan if you don't know how you will pay it back.

E. Loans - Practical Considerations

1. Debt can ruin your life.
2. A borrower is a slave to a creditor - וְעֶבֶד לֹוֶה לְאִישׁ מַלְוֶה
3. Every loan involves time, energy, hassle, stress and embarrassment.
4. Phenomenon of debt juggling/balance transfers on credit cards: This happens when people borrow to repay old loans and end up desperately trying to juggle all their debts. This is a recipe for misery.

F. Positive Loans vs. Negative Loans

1. Positive loan
   a. Definition: A loan that yields returns in the long run
   b. Examples:
      1. Mortgage (you are left with a house after you pay the mortgage)
      2. A business or investment loan (assuming the enterprise is a solid one, you should earn greater returns than the money you borrowed)
      3. Using a credit card to establish a good credit history and credit rating

2. Negative loan
   a. Definition: A loan that gets consumed with nothing left to show for it
   b. Examples:
      1. A debt to the grocery (by the time you pay your bill, you've already eaten all the food you bought - and what about next month?)
      2. Borrowing money from a friend to tide you over until your parents give you money (by the time the money comes, you have to give most of it to your friend, and then you're in a pinch once again)
      3. Borrowing money for something you can do without
      4. Installment plans for items that you'll be paying for long after the item is gone
3. The worst type of loan: Borrowing to cover ongoing expenses
   a. Ongoing expenses MUST be covered by steady income. Otherwise, you will eat yourself out of house and home - literally.
   b. If you don't have enough money: Three possible solutions
      1. Increase your income
      2. Reduce your expenses
      3. Take financial support, government aid or charity
      4. There is no other solution - borrowing is NOT an option if you can't afford to pay it back!

G. Increasing Income vs. Reducing Expenses

(Solution 3 is obviously not an optimal option) .

1. There is only so much that a family can reduce its expenditures, since people need to be able to meet their basic needs and pay their bills even if they are on a tight budget. In contrast, the potential to increase income is unlimited.
2. Budget cuts can be effective as a short-term method of attaining financial stability, but are rarely sustainable in the long term, especially when they affect the family's lifestyle significantly. Income enhancement, on the other hand, rarely shows results in the short term, but is very beneficial in the long term.
3. Increasing income is a positive, constructive step, while decreasing expenditures is a restrictive step that often causes tension and stress in the home. As

such, a family can more easily muster - and maintain - enthusiasm and motivation to increase their income than to decrease their expenditures.

4. Reducing expenses is a far more straightforward and defined step than increasing income. For instance, a family can decide to decrease their food budget by 30%, but they can't just decide to increase their income by 30%.
5. Reducing expenses provides immediate relief, while increasing income is a long-term measure.
6. Income enhancement often means working longer hours and being less available to family.

H. Psychological Aspects of Borrowing

1. Why do people buy (or charge) things that they can't afford?
2. Discussion - possible reasons:
    a. "Everyone else has it"
    b. "It's such an insignificant amount of money"
    (introduce idea of פרוטה פרוטה מצטרפת - every penny adds up)
    c. "It's a great deal"
    d. "I really need it"
    e. "I have bitachon that things will work out and I'll be able to pay"
3. Why is debt more of a problem today than it was in the past? Do people have less today?
    a. Availability of credit
    b. High cost of basic living (a car, air conditioning, summer camp, etc. can be considered basic needs)
    c. Money is virtual - you don't feel it leaving your pocket, it's just a bunch of numbers on a screen

I. Guidelines for Debt Management

Guideline #1: Divide & Conquer

Management of debt has to be separated from management of the family's income and living expenses. Loans cannot be considered income and cannot be used to cover ongoing living expenses. Conversely, money designated for living expenses cannot be used for debt repayment.

Guideline #2: Create a Debt Repayment Timetable

If the family has an annual budget surplus, it should be possible to solve the debt problem. If this amount is insufficient to cover the current monthly debt repayments, it may be necessary to procure interim loans for the family, or to renegotiate or freeze certain debts.

Guideline #3: Consolidate the Debts

The best way to pay off debt is to consolidate all of the debts into one large loan with reasonable repayment terms. The total amount to be repaid each month cannot exceed the amount that the family's annual budget surplus allows it to set aside each month.

Guideline #4: Negotiate with Creditors

If the loans that have been procured do not cover all of the debts, they should contact the creditors and suggest solutions that will ease their burden for the family. Often, creditors will prefer to be flexible with regard to the repayment terms, rather than take a chance of losing their money completely.

Guideline #5: Pay the Troublesome or Small Debts First Down to the Last Penny

Generally, interest-bearing debts, or debts that will incur late charges or legal action, should be paid first. Stress can be minimized by getting the smaller debts out of the way first completely.

Guideline #6: Get Help

There are professionals and organizations dedicated to helping people develop strategies for debt repayment. If debt is overwhelming, do not hesitate to get help.

Guideline #7: Seek Rabbinic Guidance

Borrowing money involves many halachic considerations. Before borrowing, and when making repayment arrangements, you should consult with a rav to ensure that your debt management strategies are in consonance with halachah.

Unit 7

Charity & Integrity

Goals:

- To appreciate the significance of giving charity and loans to the needy
- To establish priorities in the giving of charity
- To appreciate the value of financial independence and being a "giver"
- To examine the concept of integrity in light of current realities

A. Charity & Philanthropy: An Ethical Imperative

1. Charity is a Torah commandment emphasized repeatedly in Tanach.

> כִּי יִהְיֶה בְךָ אֶבְיוֹן מֵאַחַד אַחֶיךָ בְּאַחַד שְׁעָרֶיךָ בְּאַרְצְךָ אֲשֶׁר ה' אֱלֹקֶיךָ נֹתֵן לָךְ לֹא תְאַמֵּץ אֶת לְבָבְךָ וְלֹא תִקְפֹּץ אֶת יָדְךָ מֵאָחִיךָ הָאֶבְיוֹן. כִּי פָתֹחַ תִּפְתַּח אֶת יָדְךָ לוֹ וְהַעֲבֵט תַּעֲבִיטֶנּוּ דֵּי מַחְסֹרוֹ אֲשֶׁר יֶחְסַר לוֹ... כִּי לֹא יֶחְדַּל אֶבְיוֹן מִקֶּרֶב הָאָרֶץ עַל כֵּן אָנֹכִי מְצַוְּךָ לֵאמֹר פָּתֹחַ תִּפְתַּח אֶת יָדְךָ לְאָחִיךָ לַעֲנִיֶּךָ וּלְאֶבְיֹנְךָ בְּאַרְצֶךָ:
>
> *If there will be among you a pauper from one of your brothers in one of your gates in your land that Hashem your God is giving you, you shall not harden your hard and you shall not close your hand from your impoverished brother. Rather, you shall surely open your hand to him and you shall lend him what he requires, whatever is lacking to him... For there will not cease to be a pauper in the midst of the land. Therefore I am commanding you saying, You shall surely open your hand to your brother to your poor and to your impoverished in your land.* (Devarim 15)

2. Hashem provides for everyone, but the distribution is unequal - some people have more than they need while some have less. Why? Because He wants to give His people the merit of giving to others (*Sefer HaChinuch* 66).

> שרצה הקֵל להיות ברואיו מלומדים ומורגלים במדת החסד והרחמים, כי היא מדה משובחת... ואם לאו מצד שורש זה הלא הוא ברוך הוא יספיק לעני די מחסורו זולתנו, אלא שהיה מחסדו ברוך הוא שנעשינו שלוחים לו לזכותנו.

Hashem wished to accustom humanity in the qualities of kindness and compassion, for those are exemplary qualities...If not for this underlying consideration, Hashem would provide for the pauper without us. But in His kindness, He made us His emissaries, in order for us to accrue merit.

3. Sharing one's resources with others is not merely meritorious - it is an absolute obligation. In fact, the reason that some people have more and some people have less is because Hashem expects people to take responsibility for the poor and indigent and ensure that their needs are met as well.

   Ohr Hachaim on the verse אִם כֶּסֶף תַּלְוֶה אֶת עַמִּי - *When you will lend money to my people* (*Shemot* 22:24):

   אם כסף תלוה את עמי פירוש אם ראית שהיה לך כסף יותר על מה שאתה צריך לעצמך, שאתה מלוה לעמי, תדע לך שאין זה חלק המגיעך, אלא חלק אחרים שהוא העני עמך, ובזה רמז כי צריך לפתוח לו משלו ואולי כי רמז לו גם כן שלא יתנשא ויתגדל על העני, בראותו כי הוא הנותן לו, והוא אומרו לא תהיה לו כנושה, לשון נשיאות ומעלה, כי משלו הוא נותן לו.

   The verse "When you will lend money to my people" means: If you see that you have more money than you require for yourself, and that you are able to lend to others, you should know that this is not your portion to which you are entitled, but rather the portion of others - namely, the pauper among you. With this, the Torah insinuates that a person must open to the pauper of his [the pauper's] own resources, and perhaps it is also intimating that he should not act condescendingly or arrogantly toward the pauper when he sees that he is the one giving to the pauper. That is the meaning of the verse, You shall not be as a creditor (nosheh) to him, nosheh being related to the word for haughtiness (nesiut), for he is giving the pauper what rightfully belongs to him (the pauper).

4. When carrying out your responsibility to provide for others in need, realize that they are doing you a bigger favor than you are doing for them. For you are providing them with mere money or material assistance, while they are providing you with eternal merit. (*Vayikra Rabbah* 34:8)

> יותר ממה שבעל הבית עושה עם העני, העני עושה עם בעל הבית שכן רות אומרת לנעמי (רות ב) שם האיש אשר עשיתי עמו היום בועז אשר עשה עמי אין כתיב כאן אלא אשר עשיתי עמו.
>
> *More than the householder does for the pauper, the pauper does for the householder, as Rut said to Naomi, "The name of the man for whom I did today is Boaz." The verse does not say "who did for me" but rather "for whom I did."*

[In other words, Rut was implying that she did something for Boaz, though it would seem that he had given to her.]

B. *Maaser* and *Chomesh*: A Tenth and a Fifth

***Maaser*: A tenth**

1. From the time of Avraham, Yitzchak, and Yaakov, Jews have traditionally tithed their produce and income.
2. The minimum tithe is 1/10; the maximum is 1/5.
3. *Masechet Ketuvot* 50:

> המבזבז אל יבזבז יותר מחומש שמא יצטרך לבריות.
>
> *One who dispenses [charity] should not dispense more than a fifth [of his money], lest he become dependent on others.*

4. Exceptions to this 1/5 limitation (Source - *Ahavat Chessed* 20):
   - (a) A person on his deathbed (there's no danger that he'll become dependent on society)
   - (b) A very wealthy person
   - (c) When hungry and indigent people approach the donor for help he has to feed and clothe them
   - (d) When the recipient's life is in danger
   - (e) For the support of Torah study

5. Possible uses for maaser money
   (1) Some say it must be used for charity
   (2) Others say it may be used for other mitzvos as well; ask a rabbi

C. The Mitzvah of Lending

מצות עשה מן התורה להלוות לעניי אחינו, שנאמר (שמות כב, כד) אם כסף תלוה את עמי את העני עמך גו'. ואיתא במכילתא דכל "אם" שבתורה רשות, ושלושה מהן חובה, וזה אחד מהן. וראיה ממה שאמר הכתוב "והעבט תעביטנו" דרך ציווי. ומצוה זו גדולה יותר ממצות הצדקה, שאין העני בוש בדבר כל כך. גם שבזה תומך ידו ומחזיק אותו שלא יתמוטט לגמרי, ומקיים בזה מה שאמר הכתוב (ויקרא כה, לה) וכי ימוך אחיך ומטה ידו עמך, והחזקת בו וגו' דהיינו שיחזיק בו עד שלא יפול ויצטרך לבריות. ומצוה גם כן להלוות לעשיר לפי שעה [היינו לזמן מועט] בשעה שאין המעות מצוי לו, דגמילות חסד נוהג בין לעניים בין לעשירים. אלא דהעני קודם לו בזה, ולכך פירט הכתוב לעני במצוה זו. ואי לא דהודיענו הכתוב, היה רצונו של אדם יותר להלוות לעשיר, מפני שגם הוא ישיג פעמים רבות טובות ממנו, ועוד שהעשיר בטוח אצלו יותר. ודע עוד, דלאו דווקא הלוואת מעות, דהוא הדין דמצוה להשאיל לו כליו ושאר חפציו כיוצא בזה.

It is a positive commandment from the Torah to lend to our impoverished brethren, as the verse states (Shemot 22:24), "When (im) you will lend money to my nation, to the pauper among you...." It is brought in the Mechilta that all instances of the word "im" in the Torah relate to optional actions, but three are obligations, and this is one of them. The proof to this is the Torah's statement "You shall surely lend to him," which is a direct commandment. This mitzvah is even greater than the mitzvah of charity, for the pauper is not as ashamed [when receiving a loan, as opposed to charity]. In lending a pauper money, one also supports his hand and strengthens him so that he should not collapse entirely, in fulfillment of the verse (Vayikra 25:35), "If your brother becomes impoverished and his hand falters near you, you shall strengthen him..." meaning that he should strengthen him to the point that he will not collapse and become dependent on others. It is also a mitzvah to lend to a wealthy person temporarily, at a time when he does not have money available, for the mitzvah of chessed applies to poor and rich alike, except that the pauper takes precedence over the wealthy person; that is why the verse specified the pauper in this commandment. Had the Torah not told us this, a person would have preferred to lend to the wealthy person, because he himself can often receive benefit from him, and also because he is more confident in the wealthy person. Furthermore, the mitzvah is not limited to lending money, for the halachah is that it is a mitzvah to lend a person his utensils and other objects and the like.

D. The Torah View on Financial Dependence

1. *Birkat Hamazon*:

ונא אל תצריכנו ה' אלקינו לא לידי מתנת בשר ודם ולא לידי הלוואתם.

Please do not make us needy of the gifts of human hands nor of their loans.

2. *Masechet Beitza* 32:

כל המצפה על שלחן אחרים עולם חשך בעדו... רב חסדא אמר אף חייו. אינן חיים

One who depends on others for sustenance, the world is dark for him... Rav Chisda says: In addition, his life is not a life.

a. *Chatam Sofer*:

והוסיף רב חסדא גם חייו בעה"ב אינם חיים כי כיון שלא זכה ליהנות מיגיע כפו דכתיב גביה אשריך בעה"ז וטוב לך לעה"ב וזה הוא ההיפך משניהם. אבל ת"ח איננו בגדר מצפה על שולחן אחרים, אלא בגדר ועמדו אחרים ורעו צאנכם, וק"ל:

b. Explanation of Chatam Sofer: What Rav Chisda is adding with his statement that "His life is not a life" is that his life *in the next world* is not a life, because he did not benefit from his own efforts, as the Talmud teaches that one who benefits from his own efforts is fortunate in both this world and the next world. However, a *talmid chacham* is not considered one who depends on others for sustenance; rather, because he is engaged in Torah study, he deserves to be freed from mundane matters (see *Berachot* 35b).

3. Jewish law mandates that a person go to great lengths to avoid being financially dependent (*Tur Yoreh Deah* 255:1-2).

> לעולם ירחיק אדם עצמו מהצדקה ויגלגל עצמו בצער שלא יצטרך לבריות וכן צוו חכמים עשה שבתך חול ואל תצטרך לבריות.
>
> *A person should always distance himself from charity and subject himself to affliction rather than being dependent on others, as the Sages instructed, "Make your Shabbat a weekday rather than be dependent on others."*

4. Taking Charity on a One-Time Basis

- Student Resource no. 26: **Taking Charity on a One-Time Basis**

5. Discussion: The concept of being a "giver" or a "taker" extends beyond charitable handouts. How else does this concept apply?

E. Priorities in Charity

1. **Yourself**
   a. חייך קודמים - Your life comes first (*Bava Metzia* 62a)
   b. פרנסת עצמו קודמת לכל אדם - Providing for oneself takes precedence over anyone else (*Rema, Yoreh Deah* 251:3)
   c. "Put on your own oxygen mask before assisting other passengers"
   d. Clearly, this applies to one's basic needs, not to extravagances.

2. **Your family: Charity begins at home**
   a. וּמִבְּשָׂרְךָ לֹא תִתְעַלָּם - And to your own flesh, you shall not be oblivious (*Yeshayah* 58:7)
   b. עניי ביתו קודמין לעניי עירו - The poor of one's household [i.e., one's family] take precedence over the poor of one's city (*Shulchan Aruch Yoreh Deah* 251:3)

3. **Torah scholars** (enabling their Torah study).

> מהנכון שיהדר לכתחילה לחלקם לעמלי תורה למען יחזקו בעבודת ה' כי משמע במדרש דעיקר המעשר נתקן בשביל להחזיק לעמלי תורה.
>
> *It is proper, most ideally, to distribute charity to those who study Torah, in order that they be strengthened in their Divine service, for it is understood from the Midrash that the requirement of maaser was instituted primarily in order to support those who study Torah.*

4. **Other paupers**

   Examples of other categories of precedence in giving charity:
   (Note: This list is not exhaustive.)

   a. The needy of one's city and the needy of the Land of Israel come before other needy individuals
   b. A Kohen or Levi comes before a Yisrael
   c. Parents come before other relatives (including adult children)
   d. Food over clothing
   e. Needy woman over needy man

   See *Yoreh Deah* 251 for more details.

F. Integrity

1. Chazal tell us that the majority of people are tainted by theft (Bava Batra 165:a):

> אמר רב יהודה אמר רב, רוב בגזל
> *Rav Yehudah said in the name of Rav: Most [people are guilty] of theft.*

2. A person never profits from lack of integrity (*Sefer Chassidim*, 1075-1076).

> המלוה בריבית, ממונו יכלה, או הגוזז מעות וכן העושה עולה במשקל במדה ובמשורה ובסחורות ובכל מיני עולה, לבסוף ירדו מנכסיהם, ובניהם יתפרדו זה מזה בארץ נכריה, ונצרכים לבריות. וגם כל שיהיו חביריהם וכל הנלוה אליהם יכלה ממונם, וכל שיהיה מסייע להם.

One who lends with interest, his money will be wiped out; as well as one who embezzles money, or cheats in weights, measures, merchandise or any other fraud. Eventually, they will lose their money, and their children will be estranged from one another in a foreign land and be dependent on others. In addition, all those who befriend these [unscrupulous] people and all those who are attached to them, their money will be wiped out. The same will happen to alll those who facilitate them.

3) Discussion topics:

   i) How do you define integrity? Why do people generally view themselves as honest, when Chazal say that the majority of people have failings in this area?

   ii) Ways that people might steal without even realizing

      (1) Borrowing without permission

      (2) Copying music or written materials

      (3) Taking unfair advantage of store return policies

      (4) Taking hotel property or food

      (5) Withholding or delaying payment for goods or services

      (6) Etc.

Note: These topics are complex, and the actual halachah often depends on the circumstances.

Part 2:

Student Resources

MESILA'S GUIDELINES FOR FINANCIAL STABILITY

Charity & Financial Independence

1 Bailing people out of their financial predicaments almost guarantees that they will repeat their mistakes.

2 Although handouts, including government assistance, are necessary at times – to make sure that a person does not go hungry, for instance – it must be remembered that any time a person gets something for nothing it increases dependence and decreases motivation.

3 Accepting charity is a last resort and should be avoided if at all possible.

4 Taking charity is preferable to taking a loan without having a source from which to repay.

5 Financial independence is measured by degrees, and is not an all-or-nothing proposition. Every bit of improvement is significant.

Hishtadlut (Effort)

6 Success in any financial endeavor depends on *siyatta D'Shmaya* (heavenly assistance). But the fact that the outcome is in Hashem's hands does not absolve people of the obligation to invest the necessary effort into any enterprise they embark on.

7 From the time of Adam HaRishon, *parnassah* was meant to be difficult, and the fact that someone experiences difficulties does not mean he is doing anything wrong.

8 A person should always strive to improve his financial situation.

9 Every person has been endowed by Hashem with talents, skills or knowledge that can be used to generate income.

Risk

10 For every person, there is an appropriate level of financial risk, and it is important for every person to take certain risks.

11 There is no such thing as a no-risk venture.

Change

12 Lasting economic change happens naturally, from the ground up. It cannot be imposed on any person or community.

13 Sustainable long-term improvement in a person's financial situation is usually possible only if the person is actively involved in the change.

14 A person who does not want help cannot be helped. And no one can be forced to change his financial attitudes or habits.

15 As a means of achieving financial stability, increasing income is preferable to reducing expenditures, since reducing expenditures is liable to cause stress and friction in the home, and reductions are not always sustainable long-term.

16 Extreme financial measures do not last.

Counseling

17 A person should never be embarrassed to seek financial guidance.

18 When people are in the midst of difficult financial situations, they are often powerless to extricate themselves from their predicaments. A fresh pair of eyes is therefore immeasurably helpful.

Money & Possessions

19 Money is a means, not an end, and its importance must be kept in the correct proportion.

20 Money alone does not usually solve money problems.

21 There is no such thing as easy money.

22 No matter how high a standard of living a person maintains, there should always be things that he refuses himself and his children.

23 In any financial situation a person could possibly be in, there will be things that he will not be able to have.

Human Nature

24 People do not work with precise financial calculations; they work with estimates. And when estimating, the natural tendency is to err on the side that is more convenient.

25 Financial limitations create motivation. If a person feels limited to spending only what he has, he will be motivated to earn money so that he will have what to spend. But if a person gets used to borrowing money, his sense of financial limitation broadens to include all of the money he can potentially borrow, which decreases his motivation to earn money.

26 Financial structure creates freedom. In homes that run with a budget, money is generally less of an issue than in homes where spending limits are only loosely defined.

27 Expenses rise to meet income, because when funds are available, they find a destination. And when people's income rises, their needs rise, too – but their needs usually rise more than their income.

28 People prefer not to confront unpleasant realities.

29 The tendency is that people seek financial solutions outside of themselves, even though most viable solutions are found within their own resources.

Solutions to Financial Problems

30 Solutions to financial problems must be comprehensive, if they are to last. If even one contributing factor is not dealt with as part of the solution, the problem will likely fester and recur.

31 Flawed financial attitudes and habits are often a factor – and often the main factor – in financial difficulties, so the quest for comprehensive, lasting solutions must involve replacing these attitudes and habits with healthy ones.

32 Every person can be helped, and every financial situation can be improved, at least to some extent.

33 There are no instant or easy solutions to complex financial challenges.

34 Solutions are individual – what works for one person does not necessarily work for another.

Financial Management

35 It is incumbent upon every family to plan for their financial future and save up money to cover future needs.

36 Every drop adds up, and every little bit of money saved or earned is significant.

37 No person is perfect and no budget is perfect. Financial failure is a learning experience, not a reason to give up or abandon a budget.

38 No financial plan can be executed to perfection. But that is not a reason not to plan.

39 Financial management has to be based on the current situation as well as data from the past and future projections. But it cannot be based on nostalgia for the past or wishful thinking about the future.

40 Husband and wife have to work as a team in managing their finances and should not conceal financial information from one another.

41 Writing down budgetary data contributes to budgetary control and discipline and is a powerful financial management tool.

Children & Money

42 Children and teenagers need to have the security of knowing that their parents will provide all of their needs.

43 Children's needs are subjective, and depend very much on their environment.

44 Children do not need to know the details of what is happening with their parents' finances. The only time children should be made aware of what is happening with their parents' finances is when there is a change in the family's lifestyle that will affect them directly.

45 Money is a potent, intoxicating, and dangerous substance whose use by young children needs to be supervised and controlled.

46 The less involved parents are in their married children's finances, the better it is for everyone.

47 Supporting adult children is noble, but better than any money parents can give their adult children is the gift of financial independence.

MESILA'S GUIDELINES FOR FINANCIAL STABILITY

EXERCISE

INSTRUCTIONS: EACH OF THE FOLLOWING 20 SCENARIOS REFLECTS AN ATTITUDE THAT MIGHT LEAD TO FINANCIAL INSTABILITY. FOR EACH SCENARIO, CHOOSE ONE OF MESILA'S GUIDELINES FOR FINANCIAL STABILITY THAT YOU WOULD SUGGEST TO THE PERSON IN THE SCENARIO. NEXT TO EACH SCENARIO, WRITE THE NUMBER OF THE RELEVANT GUIDELINE.

1 | Michael needs to make some cuts to his budget. He considers cutting out the coffee that he buys each morning, but then he thinks to himself, *Why should I bother? What difference is $2 a day going to make?* ?

2 | Yaakov is worried that his friend Aaron is falling further and further into debt because of financial mismanagement, and he suggests that Aaron apply to Mesila for help. When Aaron balks at the suggestion, Yaakov goes ahead and applies on his behalf. *Once the process has begun, Aaron will cooperate*, he thinks to himself. ?

3 | Esther sees an advertisement that says: "Work from home, two hours a day, earn up to $10,000 a month. No training or experience necessary. Just call 999-5555." ?

4 | Mr. Haddad works very hard as an accountant, putting in late hours and sweating over his clients' tax returns. "I must be doing something wrong," he says. "It shouldn't be this hard to earn a living." ?

5 | Eli and Rachel are a young couple whose generous parents have given them a credit card to use for all of their expenses, with no limitations and no questions asked. ?

6 | Isaac's brother Refael is a big spender who has amassed a large debt on his credit card. Isaac decides to pay off Refael's debt in order to give him a fresh start.

?

7 | Rebecca is a secretary who is earning a bit more than minimum wage. She has been at the same position for almost ten years, and is satisfied with her job and her pay.

?

8 | Haim is worried that his wife Sheryl will be upset if he tells her the details of their financial situation. He decides not to discuss it with her at all.

?

9 | "I don't understand why I run out of money every month," Marilyn tells her Mesila counselor. "I'm earning $4,000, and spending $3,000, so why should I be having problems?"

?

10 | The Levy family decides that in order to balance their budget, they will get rid of their cars and their cell phones and will not buy any new clothing for at least two years.

?

11 | Joey opens a new business, without preparing a business plan, hiring a business consultant, or performing any market research. When his friend comments that he is being irresponsible, Joey replies, "I have *bitachon* that Hashem will take care of the business for me."

?

12 | Abe and Anita are an affluent couple who give their children whatever they ask for. "We can afford it, *Baruch Hashem*," they say.

?

13 | Maurice has been unemployed for a long time, and his savings have run out. He borrows money from a *gemach* to cover his living expenses, not knowing how he is going to pay it back. "It's better than accepting *tzedakah*," he says.

?

14 | "Just because everyone else in your class has that type of knapsack does not mean that you need it," Mrs. Gindi tells her daughter. "I grew up without it, and you'll manage just fine without it, too."

?

15 | Moshe and Elina decide that it's silly to build a budget plan, because they have no way of knowing what their financial situation will be in the future. "A person never knows what will happen tomorrow," they say. "How do we know how much we'll be earning or spending in six months from now?"

?

16 | Ben tells his neighbor Avi that he managed to build a budget plan that solved all of his financial problems. "Can I have a copy of your plan?" Avi asks. "I'll follow it exactly."

?

17 | Barbara's boss gives her an unexpected raise. "Now we'll be able to trade in the car for a newer model," she tells her husband happily. "And we'll finally be able to finish the month."

?

18 | Nathan was a successful businessman whose store was severely affected by the economic crisis, but he feels uncomfortable asking experienced businesspeople for advice.

?

19 | Mrs. Bensimon is a widow with several young children who subsists off community support. "I would love to manage without charity," she says, "but I know that's impossible. What point is there in trying to minimize the amount of *tzedakah* I take?"

?

20 | Sofia just came back from seminary and has nothing to do. "Why should anyone want to give me a job?" she laments. "I have no skills and never did well in school."

?

STUDENT RESOURCE 2

MASLOW'S HIERARCHY OF NEEDS

(MODIFIED)

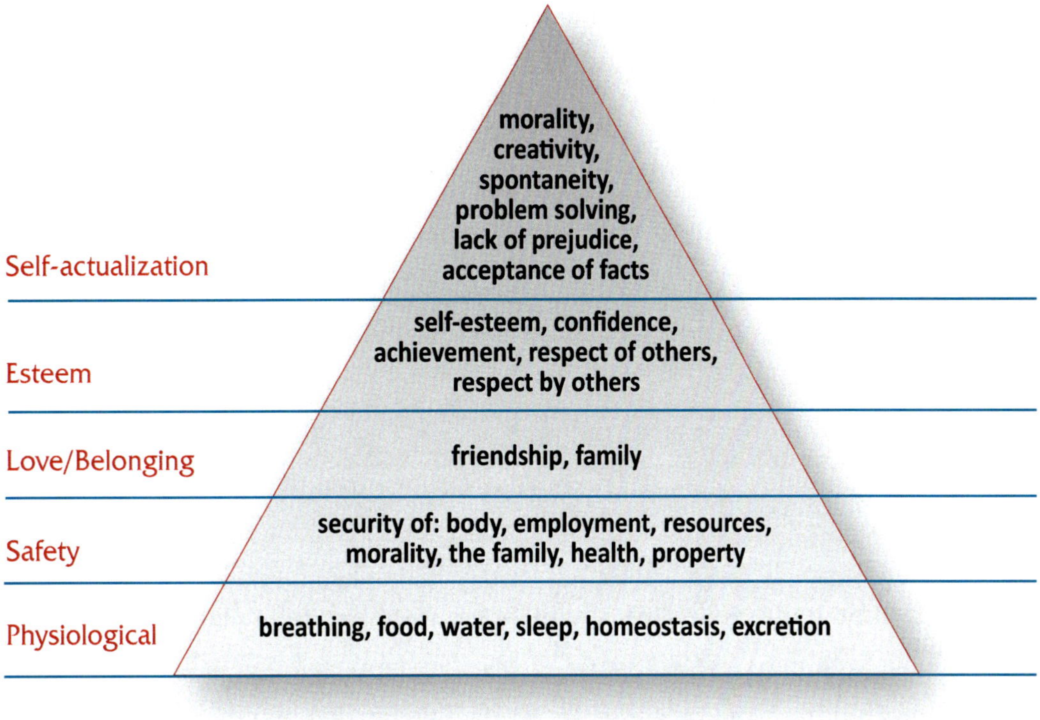

STUDENT RESOURCE 3

FIFTEEN HUNDRED DOLLAR EYE GLASSES: A SHORTSIGHTED PROPOSITION?

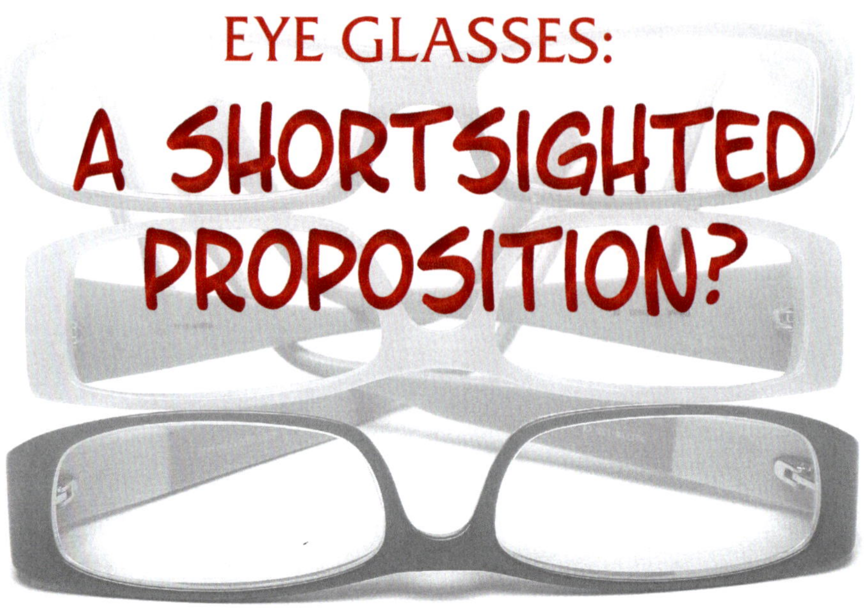

Q: I live in an affluent community, and although everyone has been affected to some extent by the economic downturn, I have not noticed any marked reduction in people's standard of living. The younger generation certainly does not seem to be feeling the pinch.

Not long ago, my teenaged son asked me to buy him a pair of designer eyeglass frames priced at $1,500. When I told him that I thought $1,500 was outrageous for a pair of glasses, he told me that his friends are wearing glasses that are even more costly. I could not argue with that – his friends have expensive taste and their parents barely restrict their spending.

Although I am not as well-to-do as some of the parents of these boys, I can afford to buy my son the glasses he wants. Should I buy them for him?

A: In a recent column, we discussed why there is a need for Mesila nowadays, considering that our parents and grandparents managed very nicely without Mesila. We said that times have changed, and the realities of today are completely different from the realities people lived with even a generation ago.

Your question is a perfect example of why Mesila is needed today. Forty years ago, even twenty years ago, this question could not have existed. But today it is an important and relevant one.

Like any *chinuch* question, this one depends on many factors, not all of which are spelled out in your letter. One factor to consider: How many of your son's friends are wearing these designer glasses – 20%, 50%, or 90%? Another factor to consider: How is your overall relationship with your son? If you say "no" to him, will he be able to accept that without questioning your love and concern for him? And a third factor: Is your son going through a difficult time in his life?

If only a few of your son's friends are wearing these glasses, if your relationship with him is generally good, and if he is not experiencing any particular difficulty right now, then there are a number of reasons why spending $1,500 on glasses might not be wise.

With $1,500, you can buy glasses for an entire family, or feed a poor family for several weeks. To spend that kind of money on glasses will either cause the glasses to take on inflated significance, or it will reduce the value of $1,500 in your son's eyes. Neither of those options represents effective parenting.

We are not saying that people who have money should not spend it on themselves. Quite the contrary – if Hashem gave you money, you should appreciate and enjoy the gift He has given you. But even when spending money that you can afford to spend, you should not go overboard and lose all perspective of the value you are acquiring with your money. What value will you acquire by spending $1,500 on glasses that you would not acquire if you spent $50, $100, or $200? Will your son see any better, look any better, or be more comfortable in these glasses? We doubt it. Chances are, the only added value you would be getting is the designer label. If so, why would you pay $1,500 to provide free advertising for a company in Paris, Milan, or New York whose merchandise is grossly overpriced?

Then there is the question of sensitivity to the community – i.e., your son's peer group. There is already peer pressure among your son's friends to wear designer eyeglasses, as evidenced by your son's desire to buy them. If your son begins wearing these glasses, it will only reinforce the trend and intensify the peer pressure on those boys whose parents cannot afford to spend $1,500 on glasses. That may be insensitive, especially at a time when the entire world is experiencing a time of economic distress.

It is always prudent to avoid conspicuous consumption (see *Biur Halachah, Hilchot Yom Tov* 529:1), but during an *eit tzarah* there is even more reason to avoid it. Flaunting the fact that you are still able to spend money freely might make you vulnerable to *ayin hara* – and this is something that cannot be remedied by tying a red string to your son's glasses.

Beyond these considerations, buying your son $1,500 glasses sets a dangerous precedent by introducing him to a level of spending that may be unsustainable. While he might be happy with the glasses now, he may be very *un*happy in the future if he has to go back to the

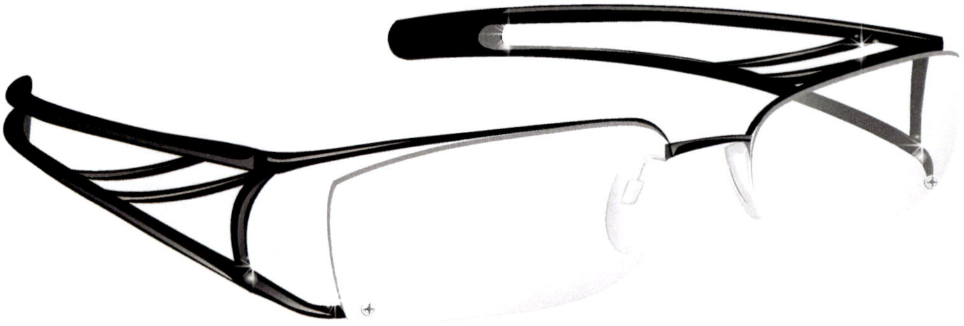

kind of glasses worn by the proletariat. And once he sees that it is acceptable to spend $1,500 on glasses, he will likely want to spend similar amounts of money on other items that he wants.

In the not-too-distant future, your son will be married, *b'ezrat* Hashem, and who knows if he and his wife will be able to keep up the level of spending you have conditioned him to? For that matter, who knows if *you* will be able to maintain this level of spending? We are not wishing hardship on anyone, but if there is one lesson to learn from the current economic crisis it is that no one's financial future is certain. Spending so much money on glasses is therefore shortsighted (pardon the pun), and might ultimately be a major disservice to your son.

Even if you were a billionaire and you could be reasonably certain that your son would always be able to afford $1,500 glasses, it would still be in your son's best interests to experience the disappointment of not getting things he wants. The Steipler Gaon said that the reason that so many people today are unhappy and depressed is because they never lacked anything when they were growing up, so they never developed coping skills to deal with disappointment. They therefore fall apart when they are confronted with life's inevitable disappointments.

Life's disappointments can be much worse than not getting $1,500 glasses, and these disappointments often happen in areas of life where money is useless. You would not want your son to fall apart if he is not accepted to the school of his choice or if he is turned down when applying for a job, and the best way to prepare him for these possible disappointments is in the training ground of eyeglasses and other minor letdowns.

The higher people's expectations are, the more likely they are to be disappointed when those expectations are not met. There is a danger, therefore, in indulging wants, whether our children's or our own. Each time we say "yes" to a child's want, we reinforce it and turn it into more of a need. Conversely, each time we deny our children something they want, we teach them to want less.

But this is true only of wants, not of needs. Needs, if unmet, only become more intense and lead to feelings of deprivation. To illustrate: if a person is hungry and does not yield to the urge to eat, he will only become hungrier, because he has a real need for food. But if a person wants chocolate and does not give in to the urge, eventually his desire for chocolate will abate and it will become easier for him to resist the temptation.

Because needs tend to intensify with time and wants tend to abate, a good way to determine whether a child's request represents a need or a want is to see what happens when you say no: is the child able to forget about the item after a few days, or does he continue asking for it incessantly?

If your son *needs* the glasses – and it is possible that he does – then you should consider getting them for him, because otherwise, he will feel deprived and his craving for the glasses will intensify. But if he only *wants* the glasses, then his initial disappointment at not getting them will fade quickly, and he will be a stronger, happier person for the experience. Stronger, because he has learned how to handle disappointment, and happier, because his expectations have been lowered and it is therefore easier for him to be content.

It is normal for children – and adults – to want things, especially things that their friends have. Before dismissing your son's request as outrageous or frivolous, it is important to understand *why* he wants the glasses and empathize with his desire. Once you understand why he wants them, you can look together for alternative ways to satisfy the hunger underlying his desire. That hunger may be for attention, for social acceptance, or for a boost to his self-image. If you sincerely try to understand your son's desire for designer glasses, you may be pleasantly surprised to realize that "yes" and "no" are not your only two options. Between $1,500 glasses and nothing, there is plenty of middle ground, plenty of room for flexibility. Another idea would be for him to shop around and try to find similar eyewear at a more reasonable price. There are many other ways to make both him and you happy – the key is to put yourself into a mindset of consideration, rather than opposition, and chances are that he will follow suit.

If you are in such a mindset, then even if you decide not to buy him the glasses, you will be able to cushion the "no" with understanding, compassion and love so that he can accept it without anger or resentment.

In summary, we recommend that you carefully consider the pros and cons of buying your son the glasses, evaluate whether his request represents a need or a want, identify the hunger underlying the request, and look for a way to satisfy that hunger without compromising your values or your relationship.

After you consider the general guidelines we have offered, we suggest that you consult with a child education expert in order to receive specific guidance for your situation.

STUDENT RESOURCE 4

THIS IS YOUR BRAIN ON EASY CREDIT

*How did Americans rack up $11.83 trillion in debt?
Short term rewards light up the brain's emotional system.*

The reward circuitry of the human brain is vital to our survival, but it wasn't built to grapple with seductive credit card offers and no-money-down mortgages. Easy credit feeds our love of immediate gratification, distorts self-regulation and diminishes prudent market behavior, creating a destabilizing positive-feedback loop. Analysts trying to understand the explosion of consumer debt should look no further than neuroscience.

The total indebtedness of U.S. households at the end of 2014 stood at $11.83 trillion, the Federal Reserve Bank of New York has estimated. That's up by $117 billion from the previous quarter. Credit card balances rose by $20 billion, auto loans by $21 billion, and student loans by a startling $31 billion. Falling indebtedness after the financial meltdown of 2008 was due largely to default rather than repayment. Now as restrictions on credit are easing, debt levels have begun to climb again

Easy credit as an economic driver has become a Faustian bargain. A market ethos that feeds on short-term desire, low interest rates and tax systems that encourage borrowing has distorted consumer choice. But more than that, it has upended the ancient survival game our brains use to weigh risk and reward.

At the core, we are instinctively selfish creatures, focused on the short term and driven by habit. The twin frontal lobes of the brain, which sit above the eye sockets, are the brain's "executive" cortex, overseeing risk assessment. Kaleidoscopic streams of incoming information are integrated there with past knowledge and instinctual drive.

A conscious, deliberative "thinking" cycle, drawing heavily on memory, runs through the outer cortex, the region predominantly concerned with punishment and control. An "emotional" circuit, focused on reward and pleasure, operates in the same region, but internally. In their crosstalk, these parallel cycles of perception and action create a balance between the fear of pain or loss and the expectation of pleasure or profit.

The illusion of continuous economic growth and the explosion of credit have thrown that balance out of whack. Thanks to the seductive appeal of today's consumer economy, perhaps for the first time in human history it is the affirmation of reward rather than the fear of punishment or failure that dominates the calculus of risk. We have become addicted to the quick fix, be that tasty junk food, the electronic cocaine of the Internet, or the painless ease of a credit card purchase.

Research demonstrates that when presented with a choice between a reward now and a greater one after a delay—for instance, $80 today or $100 in two weeks—many of us will opt for the cash in hand, despite its lesser value. Scientists call this temporal discounting. Imaging studies using MRIs show that thinking about an immediate reward lights up the brain's limbic system, which regulates emotion. Thus passion prevails over reason. That area of the brain is quieter when we're considering a reward in the distant future, and thus logic wins out. Would you rather have $80 in one year, or $100 in a year plus two weeks? The question answers itself.

Though Wall Street and international financiers have been cast as the villains of the 2008 madness, they are minor actors in the larger narrative of spendthrift habit in which we each played our part. In the past three decades, aided and abetted by the enticements of consumerism, we Americans have been busily retuning our neural architecture.

During the last 25 years of the 20th century, the U.S. economy was in recession only 5% of the time, compared with 22% of the previous quarter-century. Such long periods of uninterrupted growth reflexively foster a mood of complacency: Secure in our habits we have learned to be thoughtless. We have disrupted the autopilots of the brain's internal market, resetting the balance between hedonism and prudent self-constraint. Passion has prevailed over reason.

If we are to reset ourselves, the building of character will be key. As Adam Smith recognized, character is not born but crafted through thoughtful self-command. Ideally, over time a man becomes his own best critic, creating in the mind an intuitive capacity to monitor personal thoughts and actions. This facility Smith personified as the Impartial Spectator, moderating the perennial struggle between passion and reason.

Yet the habits of prudent concern and self-command develop, just as do profligate habits, through social exchange. Ask who is responsible for the development of character and there is no single answer, because it is a collective responsibility. It is regrettable that discussion of how good character is built has become an unfashionable subject, largely ignored in today's public debate. In such company, addicted to the short-term and too shy to consider the virtues that underpin civil society, easy credit finds its rightful place. Neuroscience suggests it's time to put impulse aside and to consider the longer view. To think for a few days before making that big purchase may offer a running start.

Questions:

1. What is the *"ancient survival game"* the article refers to?
2. In your own words what has *"upended the ancient survival game"* and how has it done so?
3. What is *"temporal discounting"*?
4. Explain: *"Americans have been busily retuning our neural architecture..."* How have our brains been rewired in recent history causing a lowering of human behavior?
5. What is *"thoughtful self command"*?
6. What is this author's suggestion to stop impulsive spending? Explain.

FINANCIAL INSTABILITY: **NO ONE IS IMMUNE**

Following is a speech given by Ike Sutton, president of an organization called the Sephardic Angel Fund, whose goal is to teach responsible budgeting habits to the community.

These are excerpts from a speech he gave at a fundraising event some years back:

Good Morning:

Thank you for permitting me to speak to you today. In the few short years that the Sephardic Angel Fund has been helping people in our community, we have learned quite a bit about the demographics and dynamics of our community.

I would like to share four main facts with you this morning about what we have learned and how this knowledge has strengthened our resolve to further our efforts. I believe that if you are informed, you too will want to be part of this opportunity to help our fellow Jews.

Fact 1:

Imagine, if you will, that there is a chart behind me. At one end of the chart, we see 10% of our community. They are the wealthiest members of our kehillah. They spend as they like and have plenty saved. May G-d continue to bless them with the prosperity they enjoy.

At the opposite end of the chart is another 10%. They are the budget-minded members of our community. They spend what they earn, whether it is $30,000 or $300,000, and live within their means. They have no debt and do not overspend in the least.

The middle of the chart represents the remaining 80% of our community. They live way beyond their means, spending

much more than they make. They are juggling 6-8 credit cards and making only minimum payments on them; they have a second and a third mortgage on their homes; and they have borrowed money from at least a dozen friends and family members.

Fact 2:

This 80% group falls into two categories:

1. those who spend to keep up with the Joneses

and

2. those who are burdened by 3 major components of their personal budgets. They are:

a. The average cost of a mortgage today is between $4,000 and $5,000 a month. Over a year's time, that amounts to $60,000 for housing alone.

b. The average annual costs for tuition and camp for a family with four children is another $60,000, maybe even more.

c. When you include an estimated cost of $20,000 per year for utilities and insurance, you are already up to $140,000—and that's after tax dollars.

That means you would have to earn at least $200,000 before taxes—and you didn't even begin to include expenses for food, clothing, medical bills, or a car. To cover those costs, you would have to earn well over $300,000 at a minimum.

At our Career Services Division, we are placing hundreds of people each year in positions with salaries ranging from $30,000 to $150,000. When is the last time you knew of someone getting a job for $300,000? Most of the people in this 80% demographic aren't qualified to land a job at even $100,000.

Fact 3: Our Youth

We took a look at a typical 18-year-old boy in our community. He has graduated from high school and figures that he can go to work and get a job for maybe $500 or $600 a week. That sounds like a lot of money to him.

He doesn't have the slightest idea about taxes. He hasn't figured out how credit cards really work. He has no experience with making or sticking to a budget.

In addition, he's not sure that he really wants to go to college because going to school for another four years means he won't be able to go to work and earn any money. And of course he needs money…

On top of all that, his parents absolutely are not cool. He can't talk to them at all about anything. They're old-fashioned, behind the times, and simply do not understand him—and they never will.

Fact 4: Newly Married Couples

Our analysis of this demographic also indicates that in four years' time these kids will be getting married, and they won't be any smarter about taxes or credit or any other issues because nobody is preparing them to be the husbands and wives, the mothers and fathers, the business leaders of tomorrow.

They have no idea about what it means to

be married. They have no understanding of the financial obligations of a married couple because they had no understanding of finances to begin with…

They lack the most fundamental information about money and marriage and being a part of a community. And of course, they haven't the slightest inkling about what it means to…raise a child together, to educate and provide everything for that child for years to come. Why? Because no one has taught them about those things either.

And that's the real tragedy. They won't be any more prepared to teach their children than their parents were. And the cycle will repeat itself over and over again.

Sounds bleak, doesn't it? It is, and it will only get worse as the community expands. Estimates are that in 25 years, our community will double its numbers. In other words, even more families will be struggling to cope, to make ends meet, to get from one month to the next, from one paycheck to the next.

At the Angel Fund, we feel we have a solution to this problem, a cure-all for this "illness," in which 80% of our community is living beyond their means.

It is not our job to tell anyone how much they should spend for their homes, their cars, their weddings, and bar mitzvahs. It is not our place to tell people how to live. If they can afford it, they are entitled to enjoy it.

In the old days, people used to walk around with coins in their pocket, and that's how they paid for whatever they wanted. If something they wanted cost 40 coins, and if they had only 20 coins, they would save until they had the coins they needed.

Today people don't have the foggiest idea about how much money they have. Their paychecks are automatically deposited. They use plastic credit cards to buy what they want without even knowing their credit limits. They can easily borrow money from the bank by putting their homes up as collateral. And it's all done electronically. They never see their money, they never feel their money, and they can never really get a handle on what they have.

Our solution is to institute a modern-day coin system, and that is called budgeting with a pencil and paper. Our first step is to make a family unit aware of what moneys are coming in and what moneys are going out. Once our family unit is aware and can actually see how their money is being spent, they can collectively address their financial problems and seek solutions.

This speech could have been given to **any Jewish community in the world** – perhaps with different numbers, but the principles are equally relevant.

The lifestyles described may be wealthy by objective standards – but do people who have more feel wealthy? Some people are struggling to pay their $5,000 mortgages the same way some poor families are struggling to pay their $500 mortgages. Mesila's tools enable people to avoid this kind of financial stress – whether they're Syrian, chassidish, yeshivish, modern, or anything else.

STUDENT RESOURCE 6

VALUES & VALUABLES

Every single hour of a woman's day is full of business decisions.
I remember when my children were small. And I had a million things to do. I did deals in my head – profits versus losses.
If they spill 6,000 Lego pieces all over the floor, but play quietly for a good hour, and it takes 10 minutes to sweep up the Lego, I've gained 50 minutes of free time....
Then there were the cumulative and non-cumulative cleaning calculations. For example, if you have an unusually busy schedule for the week, or life, what do you let go of and what not?
Cumulative chores are ones that build up. Like dishes, laundry, clutter. These will take the same amount of time if they are done immediately or left until later. Non-cumulative chores don't add up. A dirty floor takes the same amount of time to clean whether it's been dirty for three days or one.
Same sweeping motions, same time to cover floor space.
Life is a business.

From Mishpacha Magazine, Concentric Circles, by Esther Sender

Spending isn't only about money. Time and energy are other resources that we can spend - sometimes in place of money, sometimes in addition - and they also have value and need to be budgeted.

On the next page is a list of activities and pursuits that people in our communities typically devote time, energy, and money to.

Part 1:

Rank each of the following pursuits as Vital, Important, Not so important, or Not important at all.

Part 2:

Select your ten most important pursuits, and rank them in order of importance:

	Vital	Important	Not so important	Not important at all
Acquiring new skills				
Beauty treatments				
Car maintenance				
Charity				
Chessed & volunteering				
Cooking				
Correspondence (email, etc.)				
Eating out				
Exercise				
Family outings				
Family time				
Gardening				
Gift-giving				
Going to classes				
Going to Parties (weddings, Bar-Mitzvahs)				
Gourmet cooking/food decorating				
Grocery shopping				
Grooming				
Home redecorating				
Home maintenance				
Hosting guests				
Hosting parties (e.g., Sheva Brachot, parlor meetings)				
Landscaping				
Laundry				
Leisure & hobbies				
Music				
Nutrition				
Pet care				
Phone interaction with family & friends				
Photos				
Pleasure reading				
Prayers				
Recreational shopping				
Sleep				
Vacations & travel				
Wardrobe				
Weight loss				
Work responsibilities				
Other				
Other				

CHOVOT HALEVAVOT

Chovot Halevavot on Vocational Choices

חובות הלבבות שער הבטחון פרק ג'

לכל אדם יש חפץ במלאכה או סחורה מבלתי זולתה, כבר הטביע הא־ל לה בטבעו אהבה וחיבה. וכן בשאר החיים, כמו שהטביע בטבע החתול צידת העכברים, ובטבע הנץ צידת מה שראוי לו מן העוף... ותכונות גופו ואבריו ראויין לדבר ההוא... וכשן והצפורן החזקה לארי, והקרנים לשור ולאיל...

ועל הדמיון הזה תמצא מידות בני אדם וגופותם מוכנות לסחורות ולמלאכות. ומי שמוצא במידותיו וטבעו כוסף אל מלאכה מהמלאכות, ויהיה גופו ראוי לה, ויוכל לסבול את טרחה, יחזור עליה וישים אותה סיבה להבאת מזונו, ויסבול מתקה ומרירותה.

Every person has an interest in a particular vocation or type of commerce to the exclusion of others, for which Hashem has instilled in him a natural love and affinity. This is true of other living beings as well - just as He instilled in the nature of a cat to hunt mice, and in the nature of a hawk to hunt other birds that are suited to it...The physical attributes and organs [of every type of living being] are suited for [its particular sustenance]...like the strong teeth and claws of a lion, and the horns of an ox and a ram...

In this vein, you will find that people's attributes and bodies are suited to [various types of] commerce and work. If a person finds that his attributes and nature are drawn toward a particular type of work, one to which his body is suited and whose burden he can bear, he should pursue it and make it the means through which he earns his sustenance, and he should endure its sweetness and its bitterness.

STUDENT RESOURCE 8

MAKING EDUCATED DECISIONS ABOUT EDUCATION

Education – in the context of secular or career education – is a word that elicits heated reactions from many people in the Jewish community.

Some people are passionate proponents of education and career training, believing that a well-rounded, formal education is essential in order to ensure success in the workforce. Other people are equally passionate opponents of education, arguing that formal education is a waste of time for most people and poses severe spiritual hazards.

Which view is correct? Neither, actually. Education is not an objective value or goal, nor is it something that can be dispensed with entirely. It is valuable when it translates into employment opportunities, but pointless when pursued as an end in and of itself. As for the spiritual hazards along the path to education, these can be greatly minimized in most cases; nevertheless, it is always important to consult with *daat Torah* before pursuing formal training.

The right education – both initially and on an ongoing basis – is critical to success in any field. From both a Torah and a practical perspective, however, it makes sense to pursue formal education and career training only to the extent that you need it for your career. A Jew does not study any branch of knowledge – other than Torah – *lishmah*, for its own sake. Even in the secular world, people generally pursue higher education with the goal of increasing their income-generating potential, not merely for the sake of amassing knowledge.

So yes, the right education is necessary for success in the workforce – and yes, much of the formal education that people pursue *is* a waste of time, because it has absolutely no bearing on their subsequent careers.

In his bestselling book on job hunting (*What Color is Your Parachute?*, Ten Speed Press, 2011), career guru Richard Bolles writes the following: "If you are weighing a change of career, you can save yourself much waste of time on the adult folly called 'I must go back to school.' I've said it before, and I'll say it again: *maybe* you need some further schooling, but very often it is possible to make a dramatic career-change without any retraining."

In order to acquire the education that is necessary for your *parnassah* without wasting your time, you need to *optimize your education.* Career training or higher education represents an investment of time, money, and energy, and as with any investment, you have to carefully consider the returns before you invest. Aside from the money you spend on schooling, you also have to consider the lost income you will incur as a result of devoting time to your studies rather than to income-generating activity.

Optimizing Your Education

Optimizing your education means finding the most efficient educational route to your vocational destination. The need for education is very industry specific, and the type of education you pursue should depend on the type of position you are seeking to fill.

In any field or occupation, knowledge of how to do your job is a must. *How* and *where* you acquire that knowledge is usually less important.

In some fields – law or medicine, for instance – the prestige of the institution you attended is a critical factor in landing a job. In other fields, such as accounting or computer programming, all you need is to be able to show a piece of paper that says you are qualified to do the job. And in some fields, *how* you acquired your knowledge is wholly irrelevant – no one asks what school a business owner or a building contractor attended.

How formal an education you pursue should depend on how necessary formal education is to your chosen profession. You *must* attend medical school in order to become a doctor, but you don't *have* to attend business school in order to pursue a career in business. In fields that do not absolutely require formal schooling, some people are able to acquire all or most of the knowledge they need by learning from others in the field or by studying the relevant material themselves. In these fields, it makes no difference whether you receive formal education or you are self-taught, as long as you learn the right things.

Because formal education is not a goal in and of itself, it is perfectly acceptable to take shortcuts in acquiring your education. But beware: Not all shortcuts are created equal! A good educational shortcut is one that gets you where you want to go faster without compromising the education you need. A bad shortcut is one that leaves you unqualified for the position you wish to pursue.

The following are some specific recommendations for optimizing your education.

Recommendation 1:
Decide on a Career Before Going to School

In order to maximize the returns on your education investment, you need to first decide what type of work you would like to do and then find out what exactly you need to know in order to do that type of work. Sounds logical, doesn't it? Strangely, though, many, many people take the opposite approach: They pursue an education, and *then* they decide what to do! People who take this approach are virtually guaranteed that a good portion of the time and money they spend on their education will be a total waste.

Many college students give little thought to their future careers when they sign up for their courses each semester. Rather than taking courses that will give them an edge in their future work, they opt for courses that are easy, convenient, or popular. Furthermore, rather than pursuing a major in a specific area of study, they spend years earning nebulous majors such as "humanities" or "liberal arts" that have little value in the employment arena.

Career decisions are always subject to change, and as you study the material necessary for your chosen field, you may need to make some adjustments to your career plans. But we strongly encourage you to have some career plan before you embark on an education: *"Sof maaseh bemachshavah techilah."*

The sad fact is that many people pursue education and training in fields that they never actually work in. They devote years of their lives and tens of thousands of dollars to acquire knowledge and skills that they will never use! This typically happens because they did not have a clear career goal in sight when they began their education. They signed up for courses or programs because "That's what was available" or because "That's what everyone else was doing," without giving enough thought to whether they themselves were suited for the program they were enrolling in.

This approach is especially prevalent among young women who graduate seminary and are suddenly thrust into the bewildering world of job-hunting and vocational training. Having spent the majority of their lives doing exactly the same thing as their peers – going to school, going to camp, going to seminary – they approach job-hunting and vocational training with the same herd mentality: "I want to do what all my friends are doing." What they don't realize is that once they've graduated, their days of living in a herd are over. From now on, they will have to make their own life decisions and either reap the rewards or suffer the consequences of those decisions. The type of jobs and training they pursue at this tender stage in their lives will go a long way in shaping their future income-generating potential, and the more thought they put into their career choices at this juncture, the better positioned they will be to help support their families in the future.

Recommendation 2:

Experience a "Day in the Life of – "

You can't really know what it means to work at a certain type of job until you've actually observed the job firsthand or worked at it yourself. You might like the idea of working in a particular profession, but before you decide to train for that profession you should take some time to experience a "day in the life of" someone who actually works at that profession for a living.

Find someone who does the type of work you plan to do, and ask them if you can shadow them on the job for a short while so that you can see whether you'd enjoy doing what they're doing. (People are generally agreeable to such requests, especially if you offer to help them while you're shadowing them.)

While shadowing the person on-site, ask yourself, "Can I see myself doing this type of work day after day, year after year?" If the answer is yes, then you can go ahead and acquire the necessary education with the confidence that you'll be able to put your education to use in the workforce – happily. If the answer is no, then you will have saved yourself a great deal of time and heartache by discovering that you are not cut out for this type of work *before* you learn how to do it. Why wait until after you enter the field to find out the hard way that you hate the job you trained for?

A religious vocational training program was offering a two-year course in gerontology, a field whose popularity is growing due to the aging of the general population. A young woman was strongly considering taking the course, believing that she would enjoy helping elderly people improve their quality of life. Before signing up for the course, however, she spent a day in a nursing home shadowing a gerontologist. By the end of the day, she felt depressed and emotionally drained. "If I'm going to be playing ball and doing arts 'n crafts, I'd rather do it with preschoolers than with Alzheimer's patients," she said.

Some professions sound glamorous in theory, but are actually grueling in practice, and you can't know what a profession is really all about until you spend a day in the life of someone who does it for a living.

Many law students are under the impression that lawyers make lots of money and spend their days on the golf course. What they don't realize is that most lawyers never make it to the golf course, and even those who do make it there typically spend the first decade or two of their careers slaving away as junior associates, researching legal codes, writing legal briefs, and doing other tedious work for 14+ hours a day.

Recommendation 3:
Find Out What You <u>Really</u> Need to Know

Before embarking on any form of career training, find out from people who work in your chosen field what exactly you need to know in order to succeed at that field. Then, you can pay close attention to that area of study, while minimizing the time and effort you devote to areas of study that have little or no relevance to your future career. Much of what you learn formally has no practical application, and you're better off focusing on the areas that will be useful to you later on. Every course you will ever take, and every vocational textbook you will ever read, contains some material that you will never need or use, and it's wise to ask experienced people to help you filter the wheat from the chaff. For example, if you're taking a course in graphic design, find out from a graphic designer which programs you will use heavily and which ones you will use rarely or never. Then make sure to focus on mastering the programs that you *will* use.

Your goal in pursuing an education is to learn as much as you need to know in the shortest possible amount of time. That means that you should seek an education that will equip you to do the job you want to do without distracting you with subjects that have no bearing on what you'll be doing for a living.

If you are required to take courses that are not directly relevant to your future field, try to choose courses that will bring you some benefit. Opt for courses that teach practical skills over courses that teach theoretical information (for instance, data processing over ancient history, or English composition over Renaissance literature).

Recommendation 4:
Benchmark Your Education

When acquiring your education, *benchmark* (i.e., measure) yourself against accomplished people in your chosen field in order to determine what level of education is necessary to succeed in that field. *Do not* benchmark yourself against people who work in family businesses or occupy positions that they are not truly qualified for. You want to acquire an education that will allow you to be hired for your future job based on your knowledge and merit, not based on your last name, your father-in-law's clout, or any other superficial qualification. If you have acquired the right education, and you have the knowledge and skills to do the job well, you are much better positioned for success than the fellow who knows little about the job but has the right connections. And in the long run, success has a lot more to do with knowledge and ability than with externalities like family connections or prestige.

To benchmark yourself effectively, find people who are successful on their own merit, and ask them how much education they have and how much education they feel is necessary for you.

Recommendation 5:
Believe in the Value of Education

In order to make yourself qualified for the position or field you wish to work in, you have to believe that there is value in learning everything you need to learn about that field. People who believe in the value of learning are typically more patient, more thorough, and more committed to absorbing the material they study, and are more likely to remember that material when they need to put it to practical use. In contrast, people who view education as an annoying stepping stone, rather than as a valuable resource, are typically less inclined to devote the necessary time and effort to their studies, and may emerge with only cursory understanding of the subject matter.

Recommendation 6:
Become a Self-Teacher

Even if you are pursuing formal education, you have to recognize that much of the knowledge and skill you'll need for your career can't be absorbed in an academic setting – it has to be learned hands-on, on the job. In a classroom, you learn theory, and the practical application of that theory is a wholly different area of study. Classroom or textbook learning is insufficient, therefore, and needs to be supplemented by a fair amount of self-teaching.

How do you know what to teach yourself? Find mentors in your chosen field, and ask them what *they* needed to learn after they finished their schooling and began their careers. Ask them, as well, what resources they recommend for someone starting out in the field: Industry magazines? Online forums? Professional development seminars?

Self-teaching is an important component of any type of career training, but it has to be guided by experienced people in your field – educational mentors, if you will – who can tell you what to study. Depending on your personality and the type of field you wish to enter, having educational mentors might even obviate much of the need for formal schooling and allow you to become self-taught in your chosen field.

To become self-taught, you need educational mentors to help you create your own curriculum and know *what* material to study, *how* to study it, and the *proper order* in which to study it. Nowadays, you can teach yourself practically anything, with some help and guidance from people in the field.

Recommendation 7:
Make Education a Lifelong Process

Your education should not end after you complete your schooling and enter the workforce – it should continue throughout your career and throughout your life. Continuing education is critical in order to advance yourself in your field and make yourself scarcer, more marketable, and better paid. In this respect, every person has to be self-taught; it's not enough to rely on the education you accumulated in an academic setting prior to beginning your career.

Education, we might add, is not only about amassing knowledge and hard skills – it's also about acquiring the soft skills that often make the difference between a mediocre worker and an excellent one. Many soft skills can be learned, and in order for your education to be truly well-rounded, it has to include both hard and soft skills.

The Two Benefits of Education

Career education is beneficial in two distinct ways. The first and more obvious benefit of career education is that it equips you with the knowledge and ability necessary to do your job well and excel in your career. The second and more subtle – but no less important – benefit is that career education gives you confidence in your ability to succeed. And the combination of knowledge and confidence is a winning recipe.

Once you've acquired the right kind of education for your field, you can go ahead and pursue a position in your field with the conviction that you'll be able to do the job well. Whether you studied in Harvard or in your own home, if you possess the necessary knowledge and skills to succeed in your field, you can market yourself truthfully and effectively, looking prospective employers in the eye as you confidently present your credentials for the job.

Summary

Pointers for Building a Successful Educational Plan:

- Decide what you want to do
- Find an educational mentor
- Study industry specific knowledge culled from experts in field

STUDENT RESOURCE 9

THE BENEFITS OF ENTREPRENEURSHIP

There are three primary ways to earn money: through investments; through working for someone else; and through running your own business. If you have your own business, you subject yourself to the risks and vicissitudes of the business, and you absorb the profits or losses of the business. If you work for someone else, you earn a fixed salary, plus employee benefits, regardless of whether your employer does well or poorly.

There are pros and cons to both types of working arrangements, as demonstrated in the table that follows.

Note: Pros are indicated with a ☺; cons are indicated with a ☹.

Characteristic	Employee	Business Owner
Guaranteed earnings (salary)	Yes ☺	No ☹
Vulnerability to company losses	No ☺	Yes ☹
Share in company profits/dividends	No ☹	Yes ☺
Earnings limited to your level of skill, training, and experience	Yes ☹	No ☺
Passive income (possibility to earn money even when you're not working)	No ☹	Yes ☺
Freedom to do things your way	No ☹	Yes ☺
Decision-making ability	No ☹	Yes ☺
Need for salary negotiation and promotions	Yes ☹	No ☺
Ability to delegate tasks as you wish	No ☹	Yes ☺
Job security	No ☹	Yes ☺
Ability to choose your colleagues	No ☹	Yes ☺
Accountability to superiors	Yes ☹	No ☺
Freedom to walk away from your job	Yes ☺	No ☹
Ability to bequeath your position to your children	No ☹	Yes ☺

Notice that being an entrepreneur has many more pros than being an employee! Being your own boss involves responsibility and risk, but it also brings with it lots of potential advantages.

If you have already established yourself and your reputation in a particular field of employment, you should carefully weigh the pros and cons of going out on your own, rather than working for someone else. When you work for someone else, you are limited to time-based salary or wages, which may not reflect the actual value of the work you are providing. Depending on your field, your employer, and your style of work, you might be better off providing your professional services to clients directly, rather than providing those services through your employer's company or organization.

Religious People and Business: A Natural Fit

Running a business is an excellent way for a religious person to earn a living, for several reasons:

1. **Cost of education:** Earning a degree can be very costly. (A master's degree program can cost upwards of $20,000 a year.) When studying in order to open a business, however, you have the advantage of being able to study exactly what you need to know, without having to take the additional credits and core courses required by most degree programs. In addition, much of the knowledge necessary for opening a business can be acquired – and is best acquired – on the job, usually by working for someone else in a particular industry and learning the inside secrets and tricks of the trade. (This is actually true of any job: even after spending years in a classroom studying theoretical information, a person still has to acquire the practical expertise necessary to do the job right.)

2. **Time:** In many Jewish communities, young women are busy running a household and caring for their children. These realities often preclude the option of devoting significant amounts of time to extended career training.

3. **Need to earn more:** People in our communities need to earn a respectable living in order to support their families, especially since their families are much larger, on average, than those of the general population. Jobs that bring in a respectable living generally require many years of training and experience, whereas running a business usually requires minimal training and experience. Before opening your business, you can acquire only the education and experience you absolutely need, without having to present a resume to any prospective employer listing your degrees, work experience, and other credentials.

4. **Control your schedule and work environment:** As a business owner, you are your own boss, and you don't have to beg to be excused from work on Jewish holidays or Chol Hamoed, or to leave early on Fridays. You can build your work schedule in a way that accommodates your family and your religious obligations, and you can choose to work with people who share your values and set up your work environment to reflect your values as well.

Entrepreneurship and Contemporary Economic Realities

In the past, the differentiation between entrepreneurs or employees was clearly demarcated: You either had a business, or you had a job. If you had a job, you typically stayed at your job for most or all of your working life, doing the same thing for decades.

Nowadays, however, the economy is very different from what it used to be, and the line between entrepreneurship and employment has blurred significantly. Employees today no longer work for the same boss for 30 or 40 years; the workforce is a volatile place, and people switch jobs frequently. In addition, whereas in the past your typical employee worked a full eight-hour workday, many employees today have far less conventional work schedules. It is quite common for people to work at several different part-time jobs simultaneously, and it is only prudent for an employee to be on the lookout at all times for better employment opportunities. If in the past this might have been considered disloyal, today's economic realities make it necessary and perfectly understandable for an employee to be weighing his other options at any given time.

Do You Have What it Takes to be a Successful Entrepreneur?

When deciding whether to run your own business or work for someone else, you should consider the following factors:

- Your personality
- Your financial needs
- Your stage in life
- The amount of time and effort you are able to devote to your work

Of course, you also need a viable business concept, as well as a business plan, before you can think of opening a business.

STUDENT RESOURCE 10

HOW TO WRITE A GOOD RESUMÉ

Q: ***I recently saw a classified ad for a job that I think I would be good at. Now, I need to write a résumé, but I have no idea how to do that. Can you please advise me how to write a good résumé?***

A: Writing a résumé is the very first step in the process of job hunting. You should prepare your résumé even before you start looking through Help Wanted ads; this allows you to prepare your résumé properly, without the pressure of having to submit it immediately.

Your résumé, or CV (short for *curriculum vitae*), is your introduction to a prospective employer, and it determines what the employer's first impression of you will be. First impressions are often lasting impressions, and it is therefore critical that your résumé be a positive reflection of yourself and your abilities.

Your résumé is your opportunity to sell yourself, so it has to highlight your skills, talents and strengths. A résumé is *not* the place for bashfulness or misplaced humility.

A résumé should include the following elements:

› **Contact information**: Name, address, e-mail, and telephone numbers where you are easily reachable. All information should be current.

› **Personal information**: Use your discretion when deciding whether to include personal information and which information to include. Depending on which of the following are relevant (and beneficial) to your job search, you might include marital status, number of children, age, place of birth, Israeli ID number, country of citizenship, date of *aliyah*, etc.

› **Current career objective**: Briefly describe the position you are seeking and the type of company/industry you are looking to be employed by. Also indicate if you are interested in a full-time or part-time position.

› **Professional experience**: Start with your most recent job and work backwards, indicating the dates you were at each job. If you are still working, you may omit the name of your current employer; just state the type of enterprise. All previous jobs should state the name of the employer or company. Include more detailed information on the most recent position you have held (this is likely to be the most senior). Each skill that you have and job responsibility that you performed need only be mentioned once (even if you did do the same thing in five different places). Stress skills and achievements over duties.

› **Education**: List only your highest degrees and schooling. Also include courses that relate to the type of job you are seeking.

- **Languages**: If you speak more than one language, indicate which is your mother tongue. For other languages, state your level of fluency, i.e., speaking, reading, writing.
- **Computer skills**: Computer programs you are familiar with, e-mail proficiency, typing skills
- **Other interests:** This category is optional.
- **References:** It is usually sufficient that references will be supplied upon request. If you think that a prospective employer would be impressed by a particular reference that you have, then include it, along with a telephone number.

Companies generally spend less than 30 seconds reading your résumé when you first send it. If you want to get the job, you have to make your résumé stand out.

Here are some helpful tips for preparing an effective résumé:

- Keep your résumé clear and concise, no more than two pages long. A one-page résumé is the most effective.
- If you wish, you may begin your résumé with a "Highlights" section summarizing your qualifications (experience, training, significant accomplishments, outstanding skills, etc.) in a few short, bulleted points.
- In the professional experience section of your résumé, emphasize your skills, accomplishments and any supervisory responsibilities you have had. Quantify your achievements whenever possible, using action verbs in the past tense – for example, "Increased sales by 15%," "Succeeded in saving the company $20,000," "Doubled the number of customers." Don't make prospective employers infer how competent you are – tell them!
- Don't use "I" or any other pronouns in your résumé.
- Keep the format of your résumé consistent, easy to follow and pleasing to the eye.
- Make your résumé look professional. Never, never submit a handwritten résumé. If you are going to be e-mailing your résumé, make sure you save the file with a name that is intelligible and professional: "Rina Cohen Secretary Résumé", not "rc resume new".
- After writing your résumé, read and reread it carefully for spelling, punctuation, grammar and clarity. Check that all the relevant information is included and that you have not repeated yourself. It is highly advisable to have someone else proofread your résumé.
- Each time you apply for a job, tailor your résumé to fit that particular position. Emphasize qualifications that relate specifically to the job you are applying for. It helps to reread your résumé through the eyes of your prospective employer and ask yourself, "If I were him/her, would I want to hire me based on this résumé?"

- It is perfectly acceptable to prepare more than one résumé and use different résumés when applying for different types of jobs.
- If you are submitting your résumé by mail, fax or e-mail, you should prepare an accompanying cover letter that briefly describes your suitability for a specific position. This cover letter is the bridge between your résumé (the past) and your possible future working for the employer whom you are addressing.
- For people living in Israel: Prepare your résumé in both Hebrew and English and unless specified otherwise, submit both.

The above article was prepared by Mesila in conjunction with Temech, a branch of Agudah Israel of America dedicated to furthering employment in Israel.

TRANSCENDING MEDIOCRITY: **THE POWER OF SOFT SKILLS**

Why do some people remain mediocre workers their whole lives while others become superstars? Surprisingly, the answer to that question has less to do with sheer knowledge or brainpower and more to do with things like communication skills, affability, reliability, and determination.

Clearly, you need to have the necessary knowledge and professional ability – "hard skills" – in order to succeed in a particular profession, and it goes without saying that knowing more is usually better. But there's a lot more to succeeding in your field than knowledge and know-how. Many people have excellent hard skills, yet remain mediocre in terms of both their earnings and upward mobility. Generally, it's soft skills that make the difference between a mediocre worker and an excellent one.

Hard skills are the bare components that make you qualified for your profession, but they're no more than a skeleton. Just as any skeleton needs soft tissue and muscle to bring it to life, you need "soft skills" to complement your hard skills and transform them into marketability and earning power.

Before defining what soft skills actually are, let's examine three illustrations of how soft skills – not hard skills – often make the difference between successful professionals and their less successful counterparts.

Example #1:

Two skilled, experienced bus drivers, Alan and David, work for the same school and have equally clean driving records. Alan is nice to the kids, to the parents, and to the school administrators. So when the school wants to make a video to show at the school dinner, they start the video with shots of Alan picking up kids and letting them off at the school – and when the video is shown at the dinner, all the parents clap during the opening scene.

David, on the other hand, is curt with the parents when it's the first day of school and their children are worried about going on the bus for the first time. He's short with the school administration when they let the kids out of school late, and he's impatient with the children when they scream and yell and act like children. When a kid gets confused and misses his stop, David doesn't take him home, but instead takes him back to the school and lets the parents deal with it. "It's not in my contract to make extra stops," he grumbles.

Alan gets called whenever there's an extra trip or when more routes are available, while David has to beg simply to get his schedule filled. David doesn't make nearly as much money as Alan, and he feels that the school treats him unfairly.

Example #2:

There are thousands of accountants in the U.S., and one would assume that the ones who demonstrate the greatest mastery over tax code are the ones who earn more and go on to build successful firms. A closer look, however, would reveal that the highest-earning accountants are the ones who possess the ability to build relationships with their clients that expand far beyond the role of "the guy who does my taxes." These accountants become irreplaceable advisors in many areas of their clients' lives. They earn more because they are *scarce*, and most clients are not looking for a know-it-all accountant – they're looking for an accountant who's knowledgeable enough, takes their calls, and is honest, easy to work with, and attuned to the client's needs.

Example #3:

A study was done to determine why some doctors are sued more often than others, and the results of the study showed only one significant difference between doctors who are sued less and doctors who are sued more: Doctors who are sued less spend an average of 3.3 minutes more with each patient. The less-sued doctors didn't make fewer mistakes; they are neither more skilled nor more gifted; nor are they ranked higher in their respective fields. But they do give their patients a bit more time, which builds trust and rapport and translates into a better feeling on the patient's end. As a leading medical malpractice lawyer put it, "People just don't sue doctors they like."

The curt bus driver, the brainy accountant, and the brusque doctor in the above examples all have good hard skills, but are deficient in the area of soft skills. And that deficiency translates into reduced success and lower earnings.

In any field, superior soft skills make the difference between high earners and low earners. Hard skills are a necessary basis for establishing a career, but soft skills are critical – *more* critical than hard skills – in career advancement and income enhancement.

What are Soft Skills?

Soft skills are all the qualities other than knowledge and industry-specific ability that contribute to a person's professional success. Soft skills can be divided into three general categories: business skills, people skills, and personal skills.

1. *Business skills* are the qualities and abilities necessary for any type of commercial activity. Examples include:
   - Networking skills
   - Time management skills
   - Problem solving skills
   - Conscientiousness
   - Accountability
   - Teamwork ability
   - Sales ability
   - Ability to manage human resources
   - Negotiation ability
   - Writing skills
2. *People skills* are the qualities and abilities necessary for healthy communication and relationships. Examples include:
   - Empathy
   - Ability to listen
   - Sense of humor
   - Storytelling skills
   - Public speaking skills
   - Communication skills
   - Ability and willingness to educate others
3. *Personal skills* are the qualities and abilities that contribute to good character. (You might call them "good *middot*.") Examples include:
   - Resiliency
   - Reliability
   - Self-awareness
   - Integrity
   - Positive outlook
   - Cheerful demeanor
   - Confidence
   - Motivation
   - Self-discipline
   - Humility
   - Physical presentation & grooming
   - Responsibility

The soft skills listed in the three categories above do not relate directly to specific professions, nor is their usefulness limited to earning income. Soft skills are helpful in every area of life, and are a better predictor of success in any area than brains, looks, money, prestige, family connections, or any other "hard" skill or attribute.

Hard skills give you an edge on paper, but what will motivate people to *want* to work with you and to recommend you to others are your soft skills. When choosing a professional in any field, people will consistently choose the professional with the better soft skills over the one with the better hard skills.

The Journey Matters More than the Results

Sandy (Zalman) Bernstein, the late founder of the Sanford C. Bernstein investment firm used to say, "It's not only about helping clients achieve their long-term goals, it's about how they feel along the way." In other words, people evaluate an experience based more on how they felt during the experience and less on the outcome; they remember the journey more than the results.

Having a "good experience" with any worker or professional has a lot more to do with the person's soft skills than with his or her hard skills. To illustrate this idea, let's take the example of working with a contractor on a home renovation. If the contractor was abrasive, didn't return your phone calls, didn't show up on time, and caused you aggravation during the project, you are unlikely to hire him again or recommend him to your friends – even if he did a perfect job renovating your house. If, however, the contractor was friendly, responsive, punctual, and easy to work with, you'll likely call upon him again and recommend him to your friends even if there were aspects of the job that weren't perfect.

When working with people in your community, people who share your values, people you feel comfortable with – you may be tempted to overlook the importance of your soft skills and dispense with things like punctuality, accountability, appropriate dress, proper communication, and general comportment. But these soft-skill nuances are the trappings of professionalism, and often make the difference between a successful work experience and an unsuccessful one. No matter whom you're working with, it's important to make sure that your soft skills are in top form.

Soft Skills: The Bad News and the Good News

Unfortunately, soft skills are not taught in any school or textbook. You can have all the education and experience in the world and still be lacking in soft skills. That's the bad news.

The good news is that soft skills can be learned, and you don't have to pay money or invest years of your life into acquiring them. In addition, every person has *some* soft skills naturally, whether because they were born with them or because they acquired them during their upbringing. If you identify the soft skills that come naturally to you, you can build on those strengths and leverage them to become more successful in your profession. And if you identify the soft skills that do not come naturally to you, you can then work on strategies for strengthening yourself in those areas.

The key to improving your soft skills is self-awareness. You need to be able to take a good, hard look at yourself and determine what soft skills you need to work on in order to make yourself a better worker and enhance your income in the process.

STUDENT RESOURCE 12

THE SCARCITY PRINCIPLE

As with most things that have to do with economics, how much you are paid for the work that you do is determined by the laws of supply and demand. If you offer a skill set that enough people want or need, you are able to earn money. If you offer a skill set that *many* people want or need, or that people want or need *greatly*, you can earn even *more* money. And if you offer a skill set that many people want or need greatly and few other people can do, you can earn *a lot more* money. In other words, the scarcer your skills or services are in relation to the demand for those skills or services, the more you can earn. Economists call this "the scarcity principle."

Let's say you know how to flip burgers. That's something that fast-food restaurants need, and they'll be willing to pay you to flip their burgers because it seems that many people really like burgers. However, there are plenty of other people out there who can flip burgers; in fact, almost anyone with two hands is able to perform that task, so don't expect to be paid much more than minimum wage for providing that service. Your competition for the job of flipping burgers comprises most of the world's adult population.

Now let's say you're an electrician, and you know how to fix short circuits and broken appliances. Many people need this type of work done, and few people have the training, equipment, and skill and interest necessary to do it. So you can expect to be paid more to do electrical work than to flip burgers.

What if you're a doctor, and you know how to heal sick people? Everyone needs a doctor at some point, and it takes a great deal of training and skill to become licensed as a doctor. In addition, fewer people are capable of working as doctors than as electricians, which narrows the number of competitors. So doctors can charge more than electricians for their services.

Some people earn one million a year just for hitting a piece of rubber 400 feet over a wall with a wooden stick. The reason they earn so much money is that very few people can play professional baseball, and many people will pay for the privilege of watching them do it. It might seem unfair that baseball players earn more than teachers and nurses, but economics isn't always fair.

The idea is that the more rare, or *scarce*, a skill or service is in relation to the demand for it, the more money you can earn for offering that skill or service. (If there's no demand for a particular service, it's not scarce – it's simply unnecessary or obsolete. For instance, there is no demand for milkmen delivering milk door-to-door today, so a service like that would not be scarce; it would be unnecessary.)

Some professions are inherently scarce – think brain surgery or rocket science – and people working at those professions automatically command high wages. Other professions are not scarce at all – think secretaries and taxi drivers.

Scarcity is not determined only by profession, however. In fact, the Talmud (*Kiddushin* 82b) teaches that "There is no profession that does not have in it poverty and wealth." A recent illustration of this principle: Doctors in Israel went on strike some time ago to protest their low wages, arguing that the custodians in their offices were paid more per hour than the medical professionals.

The Elements of Scarcity

Scarcity is a fickle thing. A person, or even a profession, might be scarce one day, and not scarce at all the next day. For instance, before the turn of the century, there was tremendous demand for computer programmers who could tackle the dreaded Y2K bug. From January 1, 2000, however, these programmers were no longer needed. Y2K programming was no longer scarce, because there was no demand for them, and Y2K programmers were out of work.

Scarcity also has a lot to do with location. Certain people or professions might be scarce in one place, and not scarce elsewhere. Consider this story: A young woman with no teaching experience was offered a teaching job in an established community, and when she expressed hesitation about the pay, she was told, "Name your price – we'll pay it." She named a high salary figure, and the school administrator agreed to the figure without blinking. When the woman wondered aloud why the school was willing to offer her so much money, the administrator explained that all the women in the community were professionals – therapists, accountants, etc. – and there were no teachers to be had.

Similarly, domestic help is dirt cheap in some parts of the world, while in other parts of the world people pay through their noses for cleaning help and babysitting. It all depends on how many people are willing to do this kind of work in relation to how many people need it.

Clearly, scarcity is not an objective quality. There *are* certain elements, however, that drive up scarcity and thus boost income. Let's discuss these elements and examine how you can use them to your advantage.

Element 1: Skills (Hard & Soft)

Elsewhere we discussed the two types of skills – hard and soft – that make a person marketable and drive up earning power. Hard skills are industry-specific knowledge and ability, and soft skills are the intangibles and non-industry-specific qualities that contribute to success. Better hard or soft skills equal greater scarcity.

In general, the more education, training, or experience a particular occupation demands, the scarcer the occupation, and the higher the compensation. Not every highly skilled worker is paid better than every low-skilled worker, but on the whole, professionals do earn more than manual laborers.

One way to make yourself scarce, therefore, is by acquiring expertise in a marketable area. The more difficult the expertise is to acquire, and the more specific your expertise, the scarcer you will become.

While hard skills are a necessary basis for any profession, soft skills often make the difference between low earners and high earners in any field. Two people can be doing exactly the same thing for a living, and yet one is scarcer than the other because he possesses superior soft skills.

Element 2: Differentiation

The more common a skill or service, the less scarce it becomes. When a profession becomes flooded, its scarcity plummets, and the corresponding wages plummet as well. For instance, at some point graphic designers were so plentiful that they were earning less than secretaries in some places, despite their greater expertise (Element #1).

It's important, therefore, to do something that *not everyone else is doing*. The fact that "everybody's doing it" is actually a reason to *avoid* a particular occupation, not to pursue it. Don't be afraid to be creative and do something different! At the very least, if you are forced to do something that everyone else is doing, focus on ways to do it differently and better.

Keep in mind, however, that the fact that many people are already doing something doesn't necessarily mean that the profession is flooded. It may very well be flooded with mediocrity, with many people who were otherwise unsuited for the role taking it on anyway either because everyone else was doing it or because it was available and they needed a job. In such cases, there is still plenty of room for excellence in the field, no matter how flooded it is. Furthermore, the world of business is full of stories of newcomers who gained a market share previously claimed by far larger competitors who over the years grew lazy, complacent and very mediocre. This phenomenon occurs in many industries, and it allows the newcomers who set a higher standard to establish themselves quickly and profitably.

Whether you're a businessperson or a professional, an employee or a self-employed individual, you would be wise to carefully study the market and find a niche where your particular skills or products will be in demand. On the flip side, it's also wise to avoid – or at least be cautious about – offering brand new services or products, since you have no way of knowing whether there will actually be a demand for those services or products. We recommend that you look for a middle road and do something that is somewhat different from what other people are doing, but whose demand has already been demonstrated.

Element 3: Flexibility & Determination

Most people are not very flexible about what type of work they're willing to do and when they're willing to do it. There are many types of work that hardly anyone is interested in doing because the work is difficult, boring, undignified, or unfulfilling. Furthermore, people generally want to work when it's convenient, which typically means only during regular business hours (morning hours, if they work part time); only Monday to Friday; and only on workdays, not holidays. Working during night shifts, weekends, or holidays may not be an attractive prospect, but that is precisely why people who work at these times are scarcer than their colleagues and typically command higher wages.

Being flexible means being willing to do what others are not willing to do, to work under less-than-ideal conditions, and to work at times when you would rather be doing something else. Generally speaking, people are most successful doing work they enjoy under conditions that are comfortable for them. But you can't always have everything you want. Every person has to endure a certain amount of discomfort in their quest for *parnassah*, and if you are truly determined to earn a living, then you might have to take on work that you do not consider ideal – at least on a temporary basis. We are not recommending that you compromise your values or hashkafah, but we *are* recommending that you move out of your comfort zone and be flexible about what you are willing to do to earn money and when you are willing to do it. This will make you scarcer, and will increase your income enhancement prospects to enhance your income.

Improving Skills to Increase Scarcity

As we saw in Elements 2 & 3 above, hard skills and soft skills contribute to scarcity, and it follows that you can increase your scarcity by improving your hard skills, your soft skills, or both.

To do this, ask yourself the following questions:

- **Which skills, hard or soft, if added to your repertoire, would make you scarcer and more in demand?** The answer might be as simple as smiling more at your clients or coworkers or learning to be a better listener. Or the answer might be developing a creative or unusual combination of skills. A musician who can do magic tricks or acrobatics, a house painter who can do wall murals, a secretary who can type in two languages – all of these people might be scarcer than others in their field.
- **Does anyone in your field earn more money than you?** Identify those people, and investigate *why* they command a higher earning power than you. Do they possess hard skills or accreditations that make them scarcer than you? What soft skills do they possess that make them more successful than you? What would it take for you to acquire those hard or soft skills?
- **What do you see yourself doing in two years from now?** In ten years from now? How do you plan to increase your scarcity as time goes on so that your income will rise steadily, rather than remain static?

Knowing the answers to these questions will help you decide how to become better at what you already do, or expand your existing skill set and assume added professional responsibilities.

When deciding how to boost your hard and soft skills in order to increase your scarcity, make sure that the skills you focus on are *relevant* to your profession. For example, public speaking is a soft skill that is helpful in some professions, but not all. If you're a teacher or a salesperson, taking a public speaking course is likely to make you scarcer and more valuable. But if you're a computer programmer or a lab technician, public speaking ability probably won't help you much, since it's not very relevant to your profession.

Every person has many different skills and abilities, and there are endless possibilities for developing those skills and abilities. The challenge is to specialize and differentiate yourself in one specific area, rather than become a "jack of all trades, master of none."
When choosing a career or trying to advance your career, you need to focus on those skills and abilities that will make your scarcer and give you a competitive edge in your work.

STUDENT RESOURCE 13

BEWARE!

CHANGING ROAD CONDITIONS AHEAD!

DIPS, DEAD ENDS, PLATEAUS AND CLIFFS

Many people view their jobs, or their careers, as a sort of treadmill: You get on your treadmill each day, exert yourself for some time, and then bring home your wages.

In the past, this treadmill career view may have been somewhat accurate, since people typically stayed at the same jobs all their working lives. Back in the old country Yichye the spice dealer, Zecharia the silversmith and Aliza the seamstress remained at their posts from the time they came of age until they retired or passed on. Even a generation ago, people worked at the same jobs for 20, 30, or even 40 years, doing more or less the same thing every day for their entire working lives.

Today, however, the treadmills are gone, having been replaced with dizzying employment highways and corporate turnpikes. Modern economic realities such as offshore outsourcing, global freight, the FILL IN, and mega-corporations have forever altered the face of the workforce, making long-term job security a mere pipe dream.

Working, nowadays, is no longer just about *doing your work* – it's about charting a career path that will allow you to keep moving with the ebb and flow of economic traffic and equip you to consistently meet your ever-mounting expenses.

Back in the treadmill days, people didn't have to worry much about hitting a dead end in their careers. But today, practically every job evolves continually, and no matter what field you're in, you cannot realistically expect to do the same work for years on end and still manage to keep up with your expenses. Like it or not, the workforce today is a multilane highway, where survival requires navigating a maze of possible destinations, glancing over your shoulder at the competition, and scanning the road ahead for hazards.

Because plotting a successful career path involves careful planning and maneuvering, it's important to understand and identify the four types of "road conditions" that can put a damper on – or an end to – your career. Differentiating between these "road conditions" will allow you to navigate your career journey successfully and steadily enhance your income.

Road Condition 1:
The Dip

Every road has hills and valleys, inclines and dips. A good driver understands that a dip is only a temporary decline, yet knows to adjust his speed and driving style in order to navigate the dip safely and continue cruising ahead.

Every person will experience dips along the career road as well. A dip, in the career sense, is when your income is either declining or stagnating, but there is more earning potential in your field that you are not accessing. Unlike a dead end, which we will discuss shortly, a dip can be successfully navigated by making relatively minor career adjustments, and is not a cause for serious concern.

A dip can be caused by any challenge that isn't allowing you to earn as much as you could be earning or as much as others in your field are earning. Generally, it's a sign that you have to improve your skills (hard or soft), work harder, become more efficient, or even move to a different company. But you don't have to – and you shouldn't – abandon the type of work you're doing just because you're experiencing a dip.

Example #1:

A comptroller was earning $85,000 at his current job, but was stagnating at that level of income. Becoming certified as a CPA involved a modest investment of time and energy on his part, but allowed him to continue at his job at a higher pay scale, with a higher level of responsibility, thus successfully navigating his dip.

Example #2:

Robert hired Simon to work for him at a starting salary of $50,000. With time, Simon demonstrated his loyalty to the company and became more and more competent at his work. Eventually, he worked up to a salary of $60,000 as Robert 's employee. Simon was aware that people doing similar work for other companies were being paid twice as much as he was, but he knew that Robert would never pay him his true market value, simply because in Robert 's mind, Simon was still pegged as the guy who started at $50,000. In order for Simon to navigate this dip, he realized that he would have to move to a different company that would view him as the experienced professional he now was, rather than as the novice he was when he began his career.

Switching to a new company or job is a risky step, and one that must be taken with caution, since you never know how things will work out. But at times, it's the only way to successfully navigate a dip. It's something you should consider if your current job should theoretically allow you to keep moving forward, but your boss or your company is unable or unwilling to advance you.

Changing jobs is really a last resort if you're in a dip. Before you decide to take that step, you should carefully consider whether there is any way you can overcome your dip while remaining at your current post. (Note: In a dip, you might have to change *jobs*, but you should not have to change *careers*. Changing careers is something you do only when you're approaching a dead end or a cliff, as we will explain below.)

If you are in a dip, we recommend the following:

- Speak to people who are working at jobs similar to yours but are more successful and earn more. Ask them what you can be doing differently to advance yourself.
- Speak to your superiors and find out how you can improve and become more valuable to your company.
- Look inward and see what internal resources you can develop to make yourself a more valuable part of the team.
- Supplement your knowledge and skills by undergoing further professional training.

The Danger of Dips

Dips are an expected and inevitable part of any career, and are merely a sign that a slight career course adjustment is necessary. The real danger of a dip is that you might mistake it for a dead end and decide to change course entirely, instead of focusing on what caused the dip and working to improve yourself to move past the dip. Many people fool themselves in this regard, blaming their profession, their company, or their job instead of questioning what *they* could be doing differently in order to propel themselves past the difficulties they are facing.

Rachel, an administrative assistant, was having trouble getting along with her boss, whom she found to be overly demanding, inconsiderate, and volatile. After a few months at the job, she decided to quit and take a different position at a new company. But even at her new position, she had trouble dealing with the boss, who was forgetful, inattentive, and unclear about his expectations. Eventually, Rachel realized that she had simply exchanged one problematic boss for another, and that the only way she was going to succeed at her job – no matter who her boss was – was by learning to become more assertive, more of a self-starter, and more thick-skinned. This time around, she understood that her issues with her boss were a dip, not a dead end.

If you make major job or career changes when you are in a dip instead of confronting the dip head-on and working through it, chances are that you will encounter similar dips wherever you decide to go. By treating a dip as if it were a dead end, you're basically just running away from the issues that gave you trouble in the past, and those issues may continue to haunt you wherever you turn. Your next job will also have its challenges and dips, and each time you start gaining momentum you will very likely come up against the same barriers you faced in the first dip that you ran away from.

It takes a lot of stamina, hard work, ingenuity, and introspection to get through a dip successfully. It means looking inward for solutions and seeing what you could be doing differently in order to increase your scarcity, advance your career, and enhance your income. However, it's a lot easier to blame your problems on outside factors and run away from a dip. That's why most people don't bother navigating dips – they either move on to do something else or settle for mediocrity in what they're currently doing. And that's a grave mistake.

Road Condition 2:
The Dead End

When you're trying to move forward and you reach a dead end on the road, it's a clear indication that you need to make an abrupt change in course.

In the career context, a dead end happens when you've reached the maximum salary potential for the type of work you're doing and you no longer have the possibility of upward mobility. In other words, a dead end is when there's no good reason why someone should pay you more for the work you're able to do.

If you are at a dead end, and you decide that you need to earn more and advance your career, it is time for a significant career shift. (If you decide that you are satisfied at your current income level and prefer to remain at your current position despite the lack of growth potential, then you have reached a plateau, which is Road Condition #3 below.)

Example #1:

Haim, a warehouse worker, is earning $9/hour, but needs more money in order to support his family. He has reached the income ceiling for his profession, and no matter how conscientiously he performs his duties, he will remain at the same income level. If he wishes to earn more, he can learn the skills necessary to become a warehouse manager. Doing so will allow him to move past his dead end and advance his career and his income.

Example #2:

Having moved up to the post of warehouse manager, Haim is earning $25/hour, but he knows that he will not be paid more at his current position even if he switches to a different company or becomes the best warehouse manager in the world. Once again, he has reached a dead end. If he wishes to earn more, he will have to move out of the warehouse and learn additional skills that will enable him to forge a new career path.

Planning for a Dead End

The right time to plan for a dead end is well before you reach it. Dead ends don't happen suddenly; they are usually foreseeable months or even years ahead of time. If you maintain a long-range career focus, you can anticipate dead ends well in advance and plan alternate career routes that will allow you to circumvent these dead ends. Throughout your career, you should keep an eye on the direction in which your industry and your career are headed and make adjustments as needed.

As soon as you see a dead end looming, start laying the groundwork for a major job or career shift. Do some soft networking, work on improving your skills and making yourself marketable in other areas, and familiarize yourself with the latest technology and computer skills relevant to the career direction you wish to take. As with any major career change, you should consult with your career mentors in order to plan your next steps.

Will the Real Dead End Please Stand Up?

It is important to distinguish between a dip and a dead end because the two need to be handled very differently. Dips have to be confronted; dead ends have to be avoided.

As we noted above (in the section "The Danger of Dips"), people tend to mistake dips for dead ends because it's a lot easier to blame your career challenges on external factors like the economy or your boss than to look inward and work on yourself in order to grow past those challenges. But *most* career down times are dips, not dead ends, and before you decide that you have reached a dead end, you have to be certain that you have exhausted all avenues of growth and that there is nothing you can do to get past this impasse.

To ensure that you are not mistaking a dip for a dead end, you need to perform some careful introspection, both on your own and with the help of your career mentors and others around you (colleagues, family, friends, etc.). Ask the following questions: Why am I at a dead end? Where did I fall short? What have others done to transcend similar situations?

This can be a difficult conversation to have, whether with yourself or with others, for it requires you to be honest with yourself and accepting of criticism. The role of career mentors in this process cannot be underemphasized, for they are the ones who are best positioned to help you distinguish between a dip and a dead end and advise you how to proceed in order to keep your career moving upward.

Just as it is dangerous to mistake a dip for a dead end, it is also dangerous to mistake a dead end for a dip. At times, people don't realize that they're at a dead end, and they keep forging ahead until they're really stuck.

Road Condition 3: The Plateau

A plateau is actually a form of dead end, since once you reach a plateau, there is nowhere else to go. The difference between a plateau and a regular dead end is that a plateau provides certain advantages that make it worthwhile to remain there. A plateau might be comfortable; it might offer a nice view, crisp air, or a pleasant environment.

In the career sense, a plateau happens when your career has little or no potential for income enhancement, but you deem it worthwhile to remain at your post nonetheless. Upward mobility is an important ingredient of a successful career, but in some situations its importance may be eclipsed by other intangible factors, such as job satisfaction, job security, or altruism.

The following are examples of people who might decide that the benefits of their current job compensate for the lack of potential for income enhancement:

- A person who is earning enough to support his family and enjoys his job greatly
- A person who is nearing the end of his career and prefers not to make major life changes
- A teacher in a school who has achieved the maximum salary he can command, but chooses to continue in his holy work
- A person who is working in a family business and wishes to keep the business in the family

It is perfectly acceptable to remain at a plateau, provided that two conditions are met:

1. You have a compelling reason to stay at that plateau. (Fear of change or failure is *not* a compelling reason.)
2. You are earning enough money to support your family.

The decision to remain at a plateau usually involves values, not just finances, and it is therefore important to consult with a Rabbi before making that decision.

Road Condition 4: The Cliff

The cliff is by far the most dangerous road condition you can encounter on your career journey. If you do not see a cliff coming, or if you make one wrong step near a cliff – well, let's not discuss what might happen.

If a dip means that you are not maximizing your earning potential, and a dead end means that you have no upward mobility in your current career, then a cliff means that your career is about to come to an abrupt end.

In today's economy, jobs are constantly being automated or outsourced. Many careers that existed a few years ago no longer exist today, and many careers that exist today will no longer exist in a few years. If established companies like Kodak photography, Brother typewriters, and Borders bookstores could be rendered obsolete by advancing technology, so can any company or vocation that does not move with the times.

Unfortunately, many people who are in "cliff" jobs are too lazy or too afraid to learn new skills, and they ignore the handwriting on the wall that spells the end of their current job or career.

Up until a couple of decades ago, printing companies employed "strippers" to manually affix images or text to printing plates. The strippers in a certain printing company were aware of the trend toward automation, but they continued working at their jobs without exploring other options. One day, the company purchased machinery that did the work of the strippers, who lost their jobs and no longer had any marketable skills to offer.

Some industries are more cliff-prone than others. The new industries of today (hi-tech, FILL IN businesses, etc.) tend to become outdated with remarkable speed, and industries that involve repetitive, low-skilled work are easily outsourced to places where cheap labor abounds. But no matter what industry you're in, even if you think you're immune to automation and outsourcing, you have to look ahead and understand where economic trends are going to carry your job. Then, you have to adapt to the new trends accordingly and prepare yourself for the conditions of the future.

In order to avoid cliffs, you should do whatever research you can to find out where your career is headed. As part of your research, you should regularly pose the following questions to yourself, to your career mentors, and to industry experts: Where is my job headed in a year from now? In five years? In ten years? And what can I be doing in order to keep my career relevant and move myself in the same direction as the economy?

The earlier you see a cliff coming, the better positioned you are to take precautionary measures to avoid the cliff and make yourself marketable in tomorrow's economy.

The Internal Cliff

The type of cliff we have been discussing until now is an *external cliff*, one that has to do with objective factors like market trends, technological development, offshore outsourcing, etc. But there can be another type of cliff as well: You!

If your job is one that you cannot sustain as you age, you are heading for an *internal cliff*.

As people age, their physical and mental faculties start to wane. Middle-aged people generally do not have the same energy and stamina as people in their twenties and thirties, nor do they exhibit the same flexibility and drive. These shortcomings are usually offset, however, by the experience, wisdom, and good judgment that veteran workers bring to their jobs.

However, there are some vocations in which age is a definite disadvantage, and the advantages of a more experienced worker cannot compensate for the age disadvantage. These vocations typically involve one or more of the following:

- Physical exertion
- Multitasking
- High pressure
- Frequent travel
- Late or irregular hours

If you are in this type of vocation, your ability to succeed at your job might decline with time, making you eminently replaceable with someone who is younger and more energetic than you – and is also willing to accept less than you are being paid.

The Worst Time to Hit a Dead End or a Cliff

The worst time to hit a dead end or a cliff is when you are nearing middle age, after you've worked hard for quite a number of years to establish yourself in your career. At that point, you still have many years of work ahead of you, but you may not have the same energy and drive you had at 25 or 30. What's more, at that point in your life you are likely to incur some of the largest expenses of your life: paying tuition, making weddings, supporting married children, etc.

Even before you set out on your career journey, when you are in the process of choosing a profession, you should take into account the fact that your expenses will go up with time, and you should ask yourself whether you will be an appreciating asset or a depreciating asset in the profession of your choice. If possible, try to choose a career in which you will be able to keep moving upward, and avoid careers in which your value as a worker will decline or remain static over time.

Let's summarize the road conditions we discussed in this chapter.

Dips:

- Happen to everyone, at any job
- Are a sign that you have to improve yourself and your work habits
- Can be navigated successfully by making minor adjustments
- Do *not* require major career changes (although they *may* require switching jobs in some cases)
- Are often mistaken for dead ends

Dead ends:

- Happen when you've reached the maximum you can expect to earn doing what you do
- Require major career changes
- Can, and should be, anticipated well in advance

Plateaus:

- Are a form of dead end that you deem acceptable
- Sacrifice upward mobility for other intangible advantages (such as job satisfaction, job security, or altruism)
- Require careful analysis of your values and your financial future

Cliffs:

- Turn your job obsolete (external cliffs) or make you unable to sustain your job (internal cliffs)
- Are more common in hi-tech industries (due to changing technology) or in industries that involve repetitive, low-skilled work (due to outsourcing)
- Must be anticipated and planned for

STUDENT RESOURCE 14

WORKING FROM HOME **AND MAKING IT WORK!**

Working at home has numerous advantages over working in an office. It gives you greater flexibility, eliminates traveling time, and allows you to be more available to your family. It also saves you a significant amount of money in transportation, wardrobe costs, and rental of office space.

In addition, working at home can result in significant tax savings, since many home office expenses can be claimed as deductions from your income.

But there are drawbacks, as well, to working at home. For one thing, there are many distractions in a home office, such as personal phone calls, domestic tasks that need to be attended to, and interruptions by family members and visitors. It can be very tempting to throw in a load of laundry, make a quick phone call, prepare lunch, or host company when working at home. It is also difficult to juggle home and work responsibilities when all of those responsibilities revolve around the same geographic location.

In an office, there is a clear demarcation of when the workday is meant to end. Home-based workers have a harder time ending their day; they are always near their work, and there is more of a temptation to "just finish up" or take work-related phone calls at all times of the day.

Another drawback of working at home is the inherent lack of social interaction and the resulting feeling of isolation. Office environments can be conducive to team spirit and healthy competition, but these motivating factors are absent when you work alone, at home. In addition, not getting out of the house to work means that you do not get away from any stress or frustration you experience – at home *or* at work.

To avoid these drawbacks and reap the rewards of working at home, you need to create a home office environment that is conducive to success. To do this, you have to treat your work-from-home as a regular office job. An essential requirement to effectively work from home is the establishment of boundaries for both your time and your space. As in most areas of personal finance and business, being disciplined is one of the primary keys to success.

Here are some helpful guidelines:

› **Establish set times for work.** Create a realistic work schedule, and make sure that you take this schedule seriously. Make sure to start and end work at the same time every day. Without a clearly defined work schedule, the distinction between home and work can be blurred, with your work time turning into family time and family time into work time. You want to avoid the feeling that you are always at work and never at home, or vice versa. To do this, you need to have fixed work hours.

Notify your family members, friends, relatives and neighbors of your work hours, and close the door to your office and turn on the answering machine during these hours. If you respect your work time, others will, too. On the other hand, if you allow your work to be interrupted, people will find any number of reasons to interrupt your work.

By the same token, you need to respect your personal and family life, so that others will, as well. Just because you are working from home, you do not have to be always available for work. Resist the temptation of working late simply because you are working from home, and avoid the urge to answer work-related phone calls during family time.

Although it is important to avoid interruptions, it is also important to schedule break times. Take breaks that will help your productivity without distracting you from your work responsibilities.

Once you have created a work schedule that suits your needs, you can enjoy the benefits of the flexibility that working at home provides. You need to have enough discipline to stick to your schedule most of the time, but because working at home is not as rigid as working in an office, you can occasionally adjust your schedule to the demands of work or family. The key is to ensure that this flexibility works to your advantage, rather than hampering your work or disturbing your personal life.

Keep in mind when working from home that unlike a salaried position, if the work does not get done, you do not get paid. This reminder should help you to stay on track and fight the temptation to take a "quick break" to clean the kitchen or fold the laundry.

For people who "telecommute" for an employer from home, it is important to remember that using work time for personal needs is essentially stealing from the company. Workers who get paid by the hour must be scrupulous in recording their time, or work out an acceptable arrangement with their employer whereby breaks are allowed or work time is approximated.

› **Create your own office space.** Set aside a specific part of the house for your work, and keep this office space clean, neat and organized. Having a separate room that you can call your office is an advantage, but if you do not have a spare room, you can designate any area within a room to serve the purpose.

Having your own "corporate headquarters" creates a physical and mental separation between your work and your home life. It also helps others in the house to realize when you want to be at work. Your family members will quickly learn that when you are sitting in your office, you are working and are not be disturbed.

Designation of office space is also important for taxation purposes, since costs associated with the portion of your house that is set aside as workspace can be deducted from taxes.

Your office space and equipment – especially computer equipment – should be completely off-limits to children.

› **Set goals**. Prepare a list of daily tasks to attend to. Besides for your daily goals, know your long-term goals, and assess periodically whether your daily work reflects those goals.

› **Have a company name.** Instead of calling yourself, "Ilana Cohen, Graphic Artist," or "Judah Abadi," create a company name for yourself. This will boost your credibility and professionalism, which home-based workers often lack. Doing so will also lead to greater self-respect and personal pride in your work, which in turn will increase the respect you receive from others.

› **Invest in professional supplies and equipment.** Working at home does not give you license to be sloppy or unprofessional. Set up your space so that it contains all of the necessary equipment, and don't cut corners.

› **Make yourself feel like working.** Even though you do not have to leave the house for work, it is important that you look respectable and conduct yourself as though you were working in an office. Taking the time to get dressed in a manner suitable for work will make you feel more professional and behave more professionally.

› **Facilitate communication.** Because you are working remotely, make sure that there are multiple ways for people to contact you – by telephone, cellular, fax, e-mail, etc. – and see to it that you can be easily reached during your work hours.

› **Find an arrangement that works for you.** Some people can work at home with babies or young children around; others can't. Some people can tackle housework and family responsibilities while working at home; others can't. Just because you work at home, you don't have to be Superwoman. Know your limitations, and get babysitters and domestic help when you need it.

› **Get out.** To avoid the feeling of isolation, try to arrange for some of your work to be done outside the home – by scheduling meetings out of the house, for example, or by participating in professional seminars or conferences.

› **Upgrade your skills.** Working alone, at home, can make your skills rusty. Be sure to keep on top of the latest advances in your field and set aside time to continually upgrade your skills.

› **Track your performance.** As a home-based worker, you need to keep track of your own hours and expenses. Keeping careful records of all work-related income and expenses will make it easier to file taxes when the time comes, and it will also allow you to evaluate your performance.

› **Open a separate bank account.** Keeping a separate bank account for all work transactions will help you to distinguish between personal and business finances and maintain control over what is happening in each. If your work and home accounts are separate, you will be able to create budgets for both and make informed financial decisions.

Reprinted from *Your Money and Your Life: Mesila's Down-to-Earth, Torah-Based Strategies for Managing Your Finances*, by M. Heimowitz

STUDENT RESOURCE 15

LIFE INSURANCE: TO BUY OR NOT TO BUY?

By Rabbi Yirmiyohu Kaganoff

In Parshat Vayishlach, Yaakov needed to make very important and practical life decisions with major long-term ramifications, when he heard that Esav was approaching with his army of 400 men; these decisions were made based on his halachic and hashkafic background. We also have similar decisions to make. With this introduction, I bring you:

Question 1

Harry knows that, as the head of the family, he has the responsibility to care for his wife, Claudia, and their children. He feels that this responsibility obligates him to acquire an adequate amount of life insurance should something *chas veshalom* happen to him. Claudia's upbringing was that even discussing this matter can cause bad things to happen. Who is right – Harry or Claudia?

Question 2

Norma calls her Rabbi with a question. "My husband and I would like to buy life insurance, but we're concerned that it might show a lack of bitachon that Hashem always does what is best for us. Is that correct?"

Question 3

Raymond is one of the city's biggest *tzaddikim*. He teaches, voluntarily oversees some local *tzedakah* projects, not to mention his incredibly solid *keviat itim* (setting aside time daily for the learning oF Toarh). He is a *talmid chacham* and is raising his own large family. One of the professionals has offered to purchase a life insurance policy on his behalf, but Raymond questions whether doing so might jeopardize him, since his family would no longer be dependent on his support. Is his fear founded?

Answer:

At times we have heard someone opposing life insurance, claiming that it reflects a lack of *bitachon*, or that its acquisition could actually be to one's detriment. Let us understand what the halachic authorities say about this subject. Indeed, are there halachic or hashkafic concerns about purchasing life insurance? From a Torah perspective, should this practice be encouraged or discouraged?

The three situations I presented above demonstrate three different issues that rabbanim discuss when analyzing whether there is a halachic problem in purchasing life insurance. They are:

* Reprinted and adapted with permission from the author.

I. Creating a Devil's Advocate

The Talmud states (Brachot 19) that one should not say something that might cause evil to occur. *Al yiftach adam piv l'satan* – Do not create an opportunity for Satan to mix in! Is purchasing life insurance not considered encouraging the evil Satan to do something nefarious?

II. In G-d We Trust

If we really believe that Hashem provides for all of our needs, doesn't purchasing life insurance demonstrate that we are worried about the future and lack trust in Hashem?

III. Succeeding in Divine Judgment

As opposed to a human court, Hashem's judgment and decisions are perfect, and take all ramifications into consideration. The Heavenly Tribunal will not recall someone unless all the consequences of his disappearance are calculated. Based on this, perhaps purchasing life insurance jeopardizes the insured, since his family is no longer as dependent on his support, thus minimizing the merits he has when judged by the Heavenly Tribunal?

Let's analyze each one of these issues individually, in order to determine whether or not purchasing life insurance should be allowed or even encouraged.

Issue #1: Creating a Devil's Advocate

Al yiftach adam piv l'satan literally translates as, "A person should not open his mouth for Satan." One should be careful not to say something that might provide Satan with ammunition. The Talmud applies this rule to forbid a person from saying, "I sinned a lot, but Hashem has not punished me." The admission that one is guilty and deserves punishment gives Satan a chance to prosecute one in the Heavenly Tribunal. According to the *Magen Avraham*, the main concern here is that the words "Hashem has not punished me" imply that one anticipates the punishment, although this is clearly not what the speaker intends. However, when Satan prosecutes, he might take the speaker's words out of context.

The question is whether purchasing life insurance provides Satan with such an opportunity to prosecute.

A different Talmudic discussion implies that it is absolutely permissible to make arrangements for oneself in the event of one's demise, and that doing so is not considered opening one's mouth to Satan. The Talmud discusses whether someone who prepares for himself shrouds (*tachrichim*) that are four-cornered is required to attach *tzitzit* to their corners, implying that it is, indeed, permitted to prepare shrouds for oneself. In other words, planning for one's death does not constitute violating the warning *al yiftach adam piv l'satan* and does not provide the Satan with any ammunition.

Indeed, this Talmudic discussion is rallied as a source in the following situation. Maury Bond is lying on his deathbed on a hot Friday afternoon. There is concern that if he dies before Shabbat, his corpse will begin to decompose and smell unpleasant before it can be buried after Shabbat, which would not be a *kavod* for the departed. (Remember that earlier generations did not have ready access to refrigeration.) The authorities debate whether it is permitted to dig Maury's grave while he is still breathing, so that, should he die on Friday, he could be buried quickly before Shabbos. Most authorities permit digging the grave while Maury is still living; the dissenting opinion prohibits this out of concern that Maury might find out that his grave is already dug, which will distress him, and this itself could lead to his premature demise. However, none of the authorities debating this case is concerned that the efficacy of digging Maury's grave while he is still alive violates *al yiftach adam piv l'satan* and provides Satan with the opportunity to clamor for Maury's swift departure. Some of the authorities who discuss this question explicitly state that it is perfectly acceptable for a healthy person to arrange the digging of his own grave and to prepare his own shrouds, as we see from the above quoted passage in the Talmud. One highly respected authority expressly approves the practice of purchasing adjacent burial plots for a couple, the fact that at least one member is still alive notwithstanding.

Thus, we see that it is not considered *al yiftach adam piv l'satan* when a healthy person makes funeral arrangements for himself, since he is not mentioning his sins and giving Satan any reason to prosecute him. Based on this, several authorities rule that purchasing life insurance is also not a violation of *al yiftach adam piv l'satan*.

However, I would like to note that there are two sources from which it seems that *al yiftach adam piv l'satan* applies in some other cases. In *Ketubot* 8b, the Talmud states that a person should not make the following declaration, "Many will drink the cup of mourning" because of the concern of *al yiftach adam piv l'satan*. This source implies that there is concern of *al yiftach adam piv l'satan* even when one's statement does not imply that one has sinned and deserves punishment. Similarly, a different Talmud passage states that upon entering the bathhouse (which in those days involved a moderate degree of danger), one should not say, "if something goes wrong, my death should atone for my sins," because of *al yiftach adam piv l'satan*.

Thus, we need to resolve why the halachic authorities who discuss making shrouds, digging a grave, or purchasing a burial plot for a living person do not prohibit these actions because of the principle of *al yiftach adam piv l'satan*, even though the statements, "many will drink the cup of mourning" and "If something goes wrong, my death should atone for my sins," are prohibited for this reason.

The answer appears to be that these last two cases are a concern only because one is ***expressing*** the possibility of one's passing, which fits the words of *Chazal*: a person should not *say*, "I sinned a lot, but *Hashem* has not punished me." Assuming our solution is correct, arranging plans for one's demise, including writing one's will and purchasing life insurance would not violate *al yiftach adam piv l'satan*, provided that one does not express verbally the possibility of one's death.

Issue #2:
In G-d We Trust – Exclusively

A Jew is obligated to believe that although he makes an effort to earn his livelihood (*parnassah*), it is ultimately Hashem alone Who provides it. The question is whether there is a difference between working for one's daily needs and working to save money for future expenses. Is it a shortcoming in *bitachon* to save for the future? Does purchasing life insurance imply lack of confidence that Hashem will provide for his family?

To answer these questions, we must first examine the halachic relationship between *parnassah* and *bitachon*.

Is there a Dispute in the Mishnah?

The Mishnah quotes two ostensibly dissenting opinions. Rabbi Meir is quoted first as saying: "A person should teach his son a livelihood that is easy (to learn) and free of potential sin. (At the same time, he should) pray to Him Who is the source of all wealth and property. (Always realize that) there is no profession that does not have its vicissitudes. Poverty and wealth are dependent on his merit." We see that Rabbi Meir advocates teaching one's child a livelihood, while simultaneously acknowledging that livelihood comes from Hashem and not from our efforts.

On the other hand, the very same mishnah quotes Rabbi Nehorai as saying, "I abandon all means of livelihood and teach my son only Torah."

Thus, we appear to have a dispute between two *tanna'im* as to whether one should take time from teaching one's son Torah in order to provide him with vocational training. However, this analysis cannot be accurate for the following reason:

The *Talmud* teaches that Rabbi Meir was an alternate name for Rabbi Nehorai, because his teaching of Torah produced so much light. (Meir means "He who gives light," and the word Nehorai also means "light".) How could Rabbi Nehorai disagree with himself?

Resolving the Dispute

One answer to this problem is that Rabbi Nehorai's statement that he would teach his son nothing but Torah was personal – Rabbi Nehorai himself had no worldly concerns, because he placed complete trust in Hashem. Someone at this level should indeed not teach his son any worldly occupation. However, most people do not reach this level of trust and must provide their son with a livelihood, while emphasizing that *parnassah* is from Hashem.

Rav Moshe Feinstein presents an alternative answer to the contradictory statements of Rabbi Meir. The two statements are discussing different stages of life, one before the son must begin supporting his family, and the other when he has to support his family. Rabbi Nehorai's statement that "I teach my son only Torah" applies before the son needs *parnassah*. Until then, he should learn only Torah. The other statement refers to a son who has to earn a living. At that point, his father should teach him a livelihood that involves few halachic challenges and is easy to learn, while at the same time teaching him that his vocation is only *hishtadlut*, one's feeble apparent attempt, and that *parnassah* comes only from Hashem.

There is a halachic difference between the two approaches. According to the first approach, someone with total trust that Hashem will provide for him, even if he makes no *hishtadlut*, should not make any effort toward *parnassah*. According to Rav Moshe's approach, even a person with total trust in Hashem is required to have a livelihood. Rav Moshe brings evidence from several sources that it is inappropriate to rely on miracles for one's *parnassah*. Furthermore, he considers having no livelihood as equivalent to relying on miracles.

On the other hand, Rav Vozner rules, similarly to the first approach, that a pure *baal bitachon* is permitted to rely totally on Hashem for *parnassah*; however, he agrees that this applies only to rare individuals. There are stories about *Gedolim*, such as Rav Yosef Chayim Sonnenfeld, who made no conventional *hishtadlut* to attain *parnassah*. These *Gedolim*, too, must have had the same opinion as Rav Vozner. According to Rav Moshe's approach, one may not deliberately adopt such a lifestyle.

Both Rav Moshe and Rav Vozner rule that, generally speaking, people are required to have some type of *parnassah*, and that it is not a lack of *bitachon* to do so. Unless he is a great *tzaddik*, no one should assume that he has sufficient *zechuyot* (merits) to expect Hashem to provide his *parnassah* with no *hishtadlut* whatsoever on his part.

The *poskim* bring evidence from *Tosafos* that it is not a shortcoming to make arrangements to take care of one's financial future. The *Talmud* rules that although a father has the halachic ability to marry off his daughter while she is a minor, he is prohibited to do so out of concern that when she grows up, she may not like her husband. In the time of the *Tosafot*, however, underage daughters were married off, which appeared to be a violation of this halachah. Upon what basis was there a practice contrary to the Talmud's ruling?

Tosafot explains that in his turbulent times (the *Baalei Tosafot* lived during the period of the Crusades), a man who had sufficient means to provide his daughter with a dowry, should arrange her marriage to someone appropriate. If the father delayed, he risked losing his money, which could have been tantamount to his becoming unable to marry off his daughter. *Tosafot* does not contend that a person should have *bitachon* that he will have the means to be able to marry her off later.

Similarly, someone who can purchase life insurance, an annuity, or other means for making his life or the lives of his dependents more secure, may do so. *Bitachon* does not require someone to ignore future needs. *Bitachon* does require that a person realize that everything that happens is under Hashem's supervision and control.

What Will I Eat Tomorrow?

But doesn't this approach violate the statement that "Someone who has (today's) bread in his basket, and asks, 'What will I eat tomorrow?' lacks faith"? Aren't *Chazal* teaching us that someone who plans for tomorrow's livelihood lacks proper trust in Hashem?

The answer is no. This last passage is discussing people's beliefs. Everyone must believe that Hashem provides for him and that whatever happens is under His control. One may not say, "What will I eat tomorrow?" thereby ignoring Hashem's supervision. However, this does not mean that making practical plans for the future is a violation of *bitachon*, provided one fully realizes that everything comes from Hashem and is dependent on Him.

The Manna

However, there is another passage of Talmud that may indicate otherwise:

"Rabbi Shimon ben Yochai's disciples asked him, 'Why did the manna not fall for the *B'nei Yisrael* once a year (for the entire year)?' He answered them, 'I will give you a parable. A human king once provided his son with support on an annual basis. The son visited his father once a year to receive his allowance. Wanting to see his son more often, the father altered the system and began providing his son with support on a daily basis. Thereafter, his son visited his father every day. Similarly, the head of a large household worried that no manna would fall on the morrow; thus he would pray daily for sustenance." Doesn't this Talmud imply that it is better for one's livelihood to arrive one day at a time than to plan for the future?

The halachic authorities provide two answers to this question that are dependent on the dispute between Rav Vozner and Rav Moshe mentioned earlier. According to Rav Vozner, this *Talmud* reflects the ideal: A great *tzaddik* should indeed receive his *parnassah* one day at a time. However, most people are not at this level of faith and may plan for the future. According to Rav Moshe's approach, the *Talmud* means that a person should mentally acknowledge every day that Hashem provides for all his needs; however, he is permitted and required to make *hishtadlut*, which includes planning for future needs. It should be noted that all the *poskim* that I have seen discussing this issue rule that purchasing life insurance qualifies as normal *hishtadlut*.

In this context, it is worthwhile to quote a *Midrash* that demonstrates the obligation to make *hishtadlut*. Quoting the *pasuk*, "*L'ma'an yevorechecha Hashem Elokecha b'chol ma'asecha asher ta'aseh*," "So that Hashem Your G-d will bless you in all your deeds that you will perform," the *Midrash* points out that the last two words of the *posuk*, *"asher taaseh,"* "that you will perform" are seemingly superfluous, because the Torah already stated, "*b'chol ma'asecha*," "in all your deeds." What is added with the words, "that you will perform?"

The *Midrash* explains, "The Torah states, 'Keep the mitzvot.' I might think that he should do nothing and expect his livelihood to come automatically? Therefore, the Torah repeats, 'that you will perform.' If you work, you will receive blessing, and if you do not work, you will not receive blessing." This *Midrash* proves that one has a responsibility to earn a living.

Issue #3:

Succeeding in Divine Judgment

I have heard people give yet another reason why someone should not purchase life insurance. What happens if a husband does not have the personal merit to guarantee longevity, while his wife and children do have the merit or the *mazal* (fortune) to live financially secure lives? In a case like this, the husband would live a long productive life as their provider. By purchasing life insurance, which guarantees their sustenance even without his presence, he jeopardizes his life, since his dependents are now provided for should something bad happen to him.

In the one halachic source that I saw mention this concern, the author, Rav Yitzchok Sternhell *zt"l*, quoted the exact opposite approach in the name of the Shinaver Rav (Rav Yechezkel Shraga Halberstam *zt"l*, author of *Divrei Yechezkel*), who was one of the greatest halachic authorities of his day in Galicia. The Shinaver contended that buying life insurance should provide longevity. He argues that since the *mazel* of the people who own insurance companies is to become wealthy, their *mazal* will prevail and prevent them from losing money by having to pay out life insurance policies. Thus, purchasing a policy actually rallies *mazal* to one's side and does not jeopardize one's life.

Another counter-argument runs as follows: If loss of merit is a concern, then there is valid reason to refrain from accumulating any wealth. The family members of a man who ekes out a daily existence are far more dependent on their breadwinner than are the wife and children of a wealthy man, since he will leave them with an appreciable inheritance should something happen to him. Thus, one could argue that accumulating wealth is not in one's best interest, an approach that does not have too many advocates. I have never seen anyone refrain from accumulating wealth because of this concern, and neither have I seen any halachic authority suggest this as a reason to avoid affluence. Therefore, I conclude that this is not a factor in the question of purchasing life insurance.

In conclusion, I am aware of thirteen written *teshuvot* (responsa) on the purchase of life insurance or annuities, written by authorities representing *Litvishe, Chassidishe* and Sefardic approaches. All thirteen *teshuvot* permit purchasing life insurance, and some encourage the practice strongly.

Rav Meir Shapiro, the rosh yeshiva of Yeshivat Chachmei Lublin, had a very large life insurance policy, even though he unfortunately had no children. His reason was that since fundraising for the yeshiva was completely on his shoulders, he was concerned that in the event of his premature death, the yeshiva would be forced to close. We see that he was not concerned with any of the above issues and felt that purchasing insurance was an appropriate course of action. ***May we all be blessed with long years and good health.***

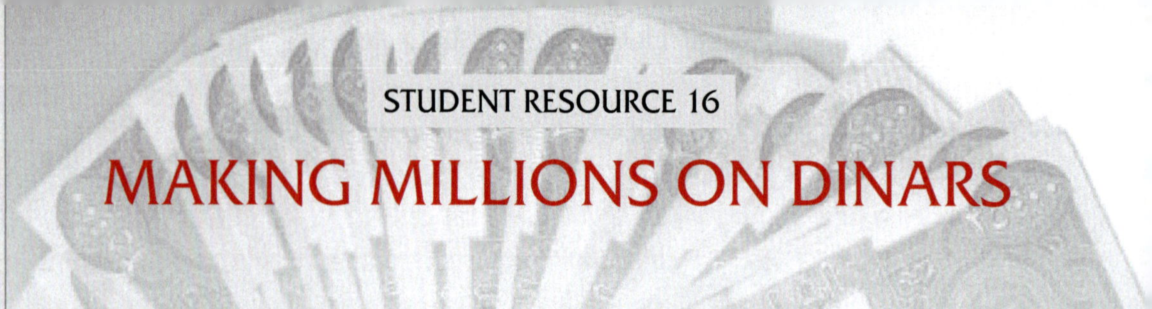

STUDENT RESOURCE 16

MAKING MILLIONS ON DINARS

Q: *A friend in the school where I learn recently showed me an article describing the exciting new possibility of investing in Iraqi dinars. The article said that until 1982, the Iraqi dinar was worth about $3, and today, one million Iraqi dinars can be bought for only $700. The value of the dinar is sure to rise when the conflict in Iraq is resolved, and my friends tell me that I can invest a few thousand dollars in Iraqi dinars and come out with millions of dollars when the dinar goes up. I have some money put aside that I was looking to invest. I have many friends who have invested in these dinars, and I am wondering if I should do the same. Do you think this is a worthwhile investment?*

A: We at Mesila are not licensed investment advisors, and we are therefore not qualified to guide you with regard to the specifics of investments. For investment advice, we suggest that you contact a licensed financial professional such as Hamodia investment columnist Aaron Katsman, who happens to be an active Mesila volunteer counselor.

We also do not wish to discuss the issue of whether it is appropriate for a *ben Torah* to busy himself with investment opportunities, although we would certainly hope that your *Yeshiva* studies focus on disputes between Abaye and Rava, not on the finer points of the conflict between the Shiites and the Sunnis.

Mesila's mission, and the objective of this column, is to convey responsible, Torah-based attitudes towards finances. We will therefore attempt to expose the fallacies inherent in get-rich-quick schemes, the Iraqi dinar craze in particular.

From the time Adam Harishon was cursed, "By the sweat of your brow shall you eat bread," earning a livelihood has been a struggle for mankind. There are no exemptions from this curse, and promises of easy money are always – *always* – misleading.

For someone learning in *Yeshiva*, investing might seem like the ideal way to earn *parnassah* effortlessly, without ever having to leave the *beit midrash*. All you have to do is put your money into a surefire investment, and you are set. Well, it does not quite work that way.

Investing, by definition, means risking capital for the sake of an anticipated future gain, or return. As a rule, return is directly proportional to risk – the greater the risk, the higher the potential return. The converse is true as well: the higher the potential return, the greater the risk. If someone promises you returns of millions of dollars on an investment of thousands, you can be sure of two things: (1) the risk is far too high to justify the investment, and (2) the person is either very naïve or a con artist.

Get-rich-quick schemes lure people with the promise of high returns and no risk. But wise investors know that any investment that cannot go down, cannot go up either. Never believe anyone who tells you that an investment is sure to go up. If it is sure to go up, there would be no risk – and without risk, there can be no significant returns.

Currency speculation is a particularly risky form of investment, because it is difficult to predict the movements of any currency, even established ones. Given the volatility of the Iraqi economy, we would not place much confidence in the prospects of its fledgling currency.

What makes you and your *Yeshiva* buddies sure that the dinar will go up? How do you know that it will not be devalued to even less than its current value? And why are you so confident that the conflict in Iraq will be successfully resolved?

Even if Iraqi dinars were worth investing in at some point, you can be sure that by the time you heard about the prospect in your Yeshiva, the market price for dinars would have already corrected itself to reflect the latest speculative excitement and the resulting demand.

"Buy the rumor, sell the news" is an old principle of investing. Basically, it means that you should only put your money into an investment before it makes the headlines, not when everyone else has already heard about it and bought in. The new Iraqi dinar has been around since 2003, and has long ceased to be the hot rumor; it is not even news anymore.

Furthermore, there is no real market for Iraqi dinars nowadays. It is therefore unlikely that you will be able to sell your dinars at a profit; you might not even be able to liquidate them at all. And because dinars are not a very commonly traded currency, you will have to pay high commissions and change fees when purchasing them. So you are basically guaranteed a loss the moment you get your hands on any dinars.

Putting your money into Iraqi dinars, or any other "can't lose" proposition, is not investing, but gambling. As such, it cannot even be considered part of your requisite *hishtadlut* for *parnassah*. You would do your friends a service by cautioning them against buying Iraqi dinars and explaining to them that there is no such thing as easy money.

Common sense would dictate that you keep your money far away from anything remotely related to Iraq, and spare yourself the pain of watching your money disappear. As for your friends who have already invested in Iraqi dinars, we hope that they lose enough money early on to discourage them from dabbling blindly in speculative investments ever again.

Having dealt with many clients who lost everything in the process of getting rich quick, Mesila strongly discourages people from investing their money without the help of an investment professional. An investment professional will assess your complete financial situation, determine the level of risk appropriate for you, and help you find the investments that are right for you.

Reprinted from *Your Money and Your Life: Mesila's Down-to-Earth, Torah-Based Strategies for Managing Your Finances*, by M. Heimowitz

STUDENT RESOURCE 17

THE MYTH OF GUARANTEED RETURNS

Question: *When I got married about a year ago, my parents and in-laws put together a nice sum of money for us to live on for several years, and suggested that I invest it. I found out about a very promising real estate project that offered 18% interest and had very wealthy, reliable guarantors offering their personal guarantee. I invested the money into that project, and for the first few months after I invested, I was able to pay my rent with the interest. Then a problem arose with the project, and for the past three months, I have not received any interest payments. I have requested that my capital be returned, but a few weeks have passed and I have not received any money back.*

I recently heard about another real estate project that pays only 16% interest, but will give me a lien on the property as a guarantee. When I get my capital back, I hope to invest in this project, but in the meantime, I need money to pay my rent. Would it be advisable for me to borrow money to invest in this second project, in view of the fact that I have a solid guarantee to borrow against? One other question – at what point would it be appropriate for me to approach the guarantors of the first project?

A: Your situation is reminiscent of Chazal's saying, *"Mi she'achal shum, yachzor v'yochal shum?" saying* – if someone ate garlic (and is suffering from bad breath), should he go and eat more garlic (*Shabbat* 31b)?

You were burned once with a real estate investment that sounded, and was, too good to be true. Even if you had more of your own money to invest, why would you take a chance of getting burned again?

As a rule, you should be wary of any investment that offers returns higher than those paid by the bank. (Government bonds are the notable exception; they pay more than the bank, but are generally considered a safe investment.)

Phrases like "guaranteed returns" and "no risk" so often dupe novice investors into naively believing that they can invest their money, and voila, their financial worries will be over. At Mesila, we see the devastating results of this naïveté time and time again.

Although we do not know the details of either of the projects you describe, we can safely assume that any investments that promise such high returns are too risky. This assumption is based on the premise that anyone looking for investment capital would prefer to borrow at bank lending rates than at 16-18%. If a real estate project is offering returns of 16% on your money, you can be sure that no bank was willing to sink money into the project. Is your tolerance for risk, or risk appetite, greater than the bank's? Considering the fact that you do not have money to pay your rent, we think not.

In our opinion, it would be unconscionable for anyone to borrow money to invest in an enterprise as risky as the projects you have described. The lien you have been offered on the second property does not guarantee anything; if the property would be enough of a loan guarantee, the bank would have been very willing to take it as collateral, and there would have been no need for private investors like yourself. Do not let the offer of the lien blind you into risking more capital, especially if the money is borrowed. If you lose the capital – and with such high risk, there is a good chance that you *will* lose the capital – how will you repay the loan?

The money you invested in the first project is not money you can count on, and definitely not money you can borrow against. While we certainly hope that you will get back your money, you should be prepared for the possibility that it may take years of wrangling and legal action before you see a penny of it.

In answer to your second question, we recommend that you approach the guarantors of the first project immediately, before they are inundated with demands from other creditors. The fact that these guarantors were once wealthy and reliable is no assurance that they will be able to bear the financial backlash of a failed real estate proposition. You should therefore make sure that you are one of the first in line to receive any money that might be forthcoming.

As a final note, we wish to stress that risking capital for the promise of high returns is not only unwise from an investment standpoint, but is problematic from a Torah perspective as well. Yaakov Avinu went back across the Yabok River to retrieve some small jugs, the Midrash tells us, because *tzaddikim* value their money. The *sefer Be'er Yosef* explains that the reason *tzaddikim* value their money is not because they ascribe importance to material acquisition; rather, it is because they understand that everything they own is a gift from Hashem, and if Hashem gives a person something, he has an obligation to take care of it and use it properly.

When people put money into risky investments, it shows a certain disregard for the *hashgachah pratit* that decreed that the money should be theirs.

In your case, the capital you invested, and now wish to re-invest, is the hard-earned money given to you by your loving parents and in-laws. *Hakarat hatov* would dictate that you should be exceedingly careful not to squander this money.

When you do get back your capital, we urge you to seek the advice of a licensed financial advisor before you invest it again.

STUDENT RESOURCE 18

SAVINGS: THE LONG AND SHORT OF IT

Question: *I earn a respectable income, and I am B"H able to support my family adequately. We live relatively simply, and I don't think that we waste money on unnecessary purchases. The problem is that we can't seem to put anything aside for the future. Besides for our mortgage, we are not in debt, but we have no savings to speak of and we never have any extra money to put away for savings. This worries me tremendously. I know that financial experts say that people should save up for retirement and other future needs, and I would love to follow this advice, but frankly, saving money just seems like an impossible goal. Do you have any ideas for me?*

A: The first step towards successfully saving for the future is having an appreciation for the value and importance of savings. Your concern over your present inability to save is a clear indication that you do possess this appreciation, and we therefore think that a bit of guidance is all you need in order to begin saving.

Saving for the future makes sense financially, but it is not only financial experts who advocate saving for the future. The Maharsha states in his *Chiddushei Aggadot* (*Niddah* 65b) that a person should put aside money for his old age. In his Responsa *Shevet Halevi* (4:1), Harav Shmuel Wosner *shlit"a* writes, "It is obvious that [for] something that is the nature of the world, such as old age or marrying off children… it is a mitzvah to prepare in advance so that he will not become dependent on others."

Clearly, then, it is incumbent upon every Jewish family to plan for their financial future and save up money to cover future needs.

How to Start Saving

Like you, many people tell Mesila that they are barely managing financially – or not managing at all – and that they cannot even begin to think about saving. But saving is not something you do when you have extra money. There *is* no such thing as "extra" money – no matter how much money a person has, there are always demands made on that money.

Saving is simply a habit. It is a habit that for some people comes naturally, and for others has to be learned. How do you get into the habit of savings? Here are some pointers for getting started:

- **Start small**. Put aside your pocket change at the end of the day, put aside $10 a week, or put aside 5% of your monthly paycheck – just save something. *Prutah prutah mitztarefet* – if you save consistently, the amounts will eventually add up. More important, saving small amounts regularly will get you into the habit of saving in a way that is almost painless.
- **Save now**. You will always have good reasons not to save. Don't let these good reasons stop you from putting away at least something. (A caveat to this pointer – if you are carrying high-interest debt –

credit card debt, for instance – your priority should be debt repayment, and not savings. A balance on your credit card might cost you 18% interest – and that's a lot more than you'll earn on most savings plans or investments.)

- **Save your windfalls.** Any time unexpected money comes your way – in the form of product rebates, tax refunds, gifts, etc. – put at least a portion of it towards savings immediately.
- **Make savings automatic.** You can set up a savings plan that will withdraw a certain amount of money from your bank account every month, or you can arrange for a portion of your paycheck to go directly to savings. This way, you barely feel the pinch.
- **Save first.** The first expense that comes off your paycheck should be your savings. Too many people say that they will save what is left at the end of the month. Those are the people who never manage to save anything.
- **Make it a team effort.** Both husband and wife – and possibly children as well, depending on their ages – need to be actively involved in the savings habit in order for it to work.
- **Watch where the money goes.** People who keep track of where their money goes end up spending less and saving more. Knowing how you are spending your money gives you more control over your expenditures and helps you to make better spending decisions. This leaves you with more money to save. It also gives you the freedom to decide how to use your money, rather than allowing spending pressures to dictate where your money goes.

Once you have decided to start saving, the next step is to decide what to do with your savings. There are two important categories of savings: short-term and long-term. Each of these requires a different strategy.

Short-Term Savings

This is the money you'll need for emergencies and for foreseeable large expenses.

Everyone needs some short-term savings. If you don't have any short-term savings, even minor financial setbacks can have disastrous results. A burst pipe, or even something as predictable as summer camp, can land you in debt or force you to sell or forfeit some of your assets. You would not want to lose your house or your car because you are temporarily unable to make the payments.

Short-term savings can earn enough interest to keep up with inflation, but will never yield the high returns associated with higher-risk investments. When choosing a home for your short-term savings, your primary considerations should be accessibility, liquidity and safety of principal.

Where should you keep your short-term savings? In a place that is accessible enough to dip into in a time of real need yet not accessible enough to spend any time you run out of cash. We recommend that you put short-term savings in a separate bank account, in a trustworthy *gemach*, or in very low-risk investments such as money market accounts, money market funds, certificates of deposit, high-interest savings accounts (available at certain banks and financial institutions) or treasury bonds. Each of these options has its pros and cons, but all of them are relatively safe, relatively liquid (easy to convert to cash), and earn relatively low interest.

Your should *not* put your short-term savings in higher-risk investments such as stocks, commodities or real estate.

How much money should you keep in short-term savings? That depends on your situation and your family's needs. Financial professionals usually recommend setting aside at least three months' worth of living expenses to tide you over in the event of an emergency or temporary unemployment or disability.

Besides for this emergency fund, you should also save for expenses looming on the horizon: your annual car insurance bill, the sputtering refrigerator that will need to be replaced soon, your son's bar mitzvah, and so on. These expenses are all predictable, and you have two choices how to pay for them: save up money and *earn* interest, or borrow the money and *pay* interest (at a much higher rate).

Long-Term Savings

Long-term savings is the money you'll need for times of considerable financial strain, such as marrying off children and old age.

When choosing a home for your long-term savings, remember that inflation reduces the value of your money by about 3% a year. By keeping your long-term savings under your mattress, you actually lose money. It is therefore important to put your money in a place where it will earn respectable returns. That is why the term "investing" is used much more with regard to long-term savings than with regard to short-term savings.

With long-term savings, you have the opportunity to let your investments earn compound interest (interest on interest), which effortlessly multiplies your investment. But compound interest needs time to work its magic.

To illustrate: If you save $2,000 a year for 40 years (a total savings of $80,000) and earn interest of 8% annually, you will have $559,562 by the time you are finished. If you save $2,000 a year for 30 years (a total savings of $60,000) at the same interest rate of 8%, you will end up with $244,692 – less than half. (For comparison's sake, saving the same amount at an interest rate of 5% would give you $253,680 after 40 years and $139,522 after 30 years.)

Here's another example. Let's say you want to save about $50,000 for your son's wedding. If your son is a newborn, you need to save $100 a month at 8% for 18 years (a total savings of $21,600) to have that amount. If your son is 13, you will need to save $430 a month for 7 years at 8% (a total savings of $36,120) to have that same $50,000 by the time he turns 20.

People in their 20s don't usually think much about marrying off their children or about their retirement, but if they would, they would reap the rewards later. When you are young, you can invest relatively little and wind up with far more money than someone older who saves much more.

The simplest way to start saving for retirement is to sign up for your employer's pension plan (known as a 401(k) in the U.S.). If this is not an option, you should speak to a financial adviser about starting your own tax-deferred savings plan (known as an IRA in the U.S.). People in Israel should speak to an insurance agent who specializes in pension planning.

Putting money into stocks and stock funds – a terrible idea for short-term savings – is actually a very good idea for long-term savings. The stock market is notorious for its volatility, but over the past 80 years it has yielded an average return of about 10% – higher than any other type of investment.

Another advantage of the stock market is that you have the option of investing even minimal amounts. Even if you cannot afford to put away a lot of money, you can still enjoy the long-term benefits of stock market investments.

Higher returns like those associated with the stock market usually involve higher risks. When you are investing for the long term, however, you are able to accept more risk. Since time is on your side, you have the ability to ride out the ups and downs of the economy without being affected every time the market takes a hit.

When investing in the stock market, we strongly discourage active investing or day trading. The approach we advocate is "buy and hold," in which you allow your portfolio to grow over time without selling or exchanging specific investments.

To minimize your risks, it is important to maintain a diversified investment portfolio. This is in keeping with Chazal's advice (*Bava Metzia* 42b) to keep a third of your assets in real estate, a third in merchandise, and a third liquid.

Diversification ensures that your financial future is not dependent on the performance of any one investment. Mutual funds (including index funds and retirement funds) are a common type of diversified investment, although not all mutual funds are created equal.

A good investment portfolio contains a mixture of stocks, bonds and real estate investments. The exact mixture should be determined based on your level of risk tolerance, which depends on factors such as your present financial situation, your future financial goals, and the age and number of your dependents. We recommend that you work with a licensed financial advisor to decide what types of investments are appropriate for you.

As you approach the time when you are going to need to withdraw money from long-term savings, financial experts recommend that you shift some of your holdings into bonds, which are considered less profitable but also less volatile than stocks. In this way, you are protected if the stock market suddenly crashes just before you need to dip into your savings.

In comparison to stocks and bonds, certain real estate and business investments require a much larger initial outlay and a far more sophisticated investment strategy. Novice investors should steer clear of these types of investments, which necessitate professional evaluation, extensive research, a thorough understanding of the market, and a high level of risk tolerance.

Once you have started a long-term savings plan, stick with it. There will always be new investment possibilities on the horizon that sound more exciting and promise higher returns, but in the end, the simple, steady and boring usually outperforms the new, exciting and lucrative.

It's never too late – or too early – to start saving for the future. The key is to determine what your savings goals are, and to start – today!

Reprinted from *Your Money and Your Life: Mesila's Down-to-Earth, Torah-Based Strategies for Managing Your Finances*, by M. Heimowitz

THE MAGIC OF COMPOUND INTEREST
OR
THE TIME VALUE OF MONEY

Once upon a time, Jaclyn and Jill were 17-year-old twin sisters in high school who did a lot of babysitting in their spare time. Their grandmother promised to match any money they saved up in an IRA (IRA: A personal retirement plan that enjoys special tax benefits), which was paying 7.5% compound interest (don't forget, this is a fairy tale).

Jaclyn managed to put aside $600 a year, which her grandmother matched, for a total of $1200, and they continued this arrangement for 10 years.

Jill, in the meantime, drank a lot of iced coffee. When she decided to cut down on caffeine 10 years later, at age 27, she found herself with some extra cash, and she too began to take advantage of Grandma's largesse. She opened her own IRA and put away $1200 for the next 24 years, until Grandma passed away.

At that point, Jaclyn and Jill decided to take a peek at their accounts and see how much money was in there.

Table A

At age	Jaclyn saves	Jill saves
17	$1200	$0
18	$1200	$0
19	$1200	$0
20	$1200	$0
21	$1200	$0
22	$1200	$0
23	$1200	$0
24	$1200	$0
25	$1200	$0
26	$1200	$0

Table B

At age	If Jaclyn stops saving	If Jaclyn continues saving	Jill starts saving
27	$0	$1200	$1200
28	$0	$1200	$1200
29	$0	$1200	$1200
30	$0	$1200	$1200
31	$0	$1200	$1200
32	$0	$1200	$1200
33	$0	$1200	$1200
34	$0	$1200	$1200
35	$0	$1200	$1200
36	$0	$1200	$1200
37	$0	$1200	$1200
38	$0	$1200	$1200
39	$0	$1200	$1200
40	$0	$1200	$1200
41	$0	$1200	$1200
42	$0	$1200	$1200
43	$0	$1200	$1200
44	$0	$1200	$1200
45	$0	$1200	$1200
46	$0	$1200	$1200
47	$0	$1200	$1200
48	$0	$1200	$1200
49	$0	$1200	$1200
50	$0	$1200	$1200
Total IRA contribution:	$12,000	$40,000	$28,000
Total account value:	**$96,307**	**$169,872**	**$73,566**

Look at what happened:

Jaclyn 's contribution in the first 10 years, totaling $12,000, grows to $96,307 by age 50 – even if she stops contributing at age 26. Jill, who begins investing at age 27, contributes a total of $28,000 over 24 years, but her account value at age 50 is still less than Jaclyn 's. Jill contributed more than twice as much money but still hasn't caught up with Jaclyn – all because she procrastinated. The story of Jaclyn and Jill illustrates the magic of compounding interest, or the time value of money.

Our example uses an IRA as a savings plan, but the principle is true regardless of what type of investment account you have. The moral of the story: Start saving *now*.

STUDENT RESOURCE 20

HETER ISKA FORM FOR BUSINESS LOANS

sample

The undersigned ______________________________ ("the Manager")

acknowledges receipt of $ ______________________ ("the Funds")

from ______________________________________ ("the Investor")

The Manager obligates himself to invest the amount of the Funds on behalf of the Investor in a ny investment or to assign to the Investor a proportionate share of the Manager's assets. If the Manager pays the Investor a return equal to   % per annum on the Funds together with an amount equal to the Investor's usual fees, benefits, and charges for providing funds if applicable (collectively called "the Yield"), and repays the Funds in accordance with and at the times stipulated in the attached Schedule and pays the full amount of the Funds and any accrued and unpaid Yield, to be fully paid to the Investor by the Maturity date __________, then the Manager shall not be obligated to provide to the Investor any accounting of profits or losses and the Manager shall be entitled to retain all profits in excess of the Yield as the Manager's compensation. The Manager will notify the Investor, in writing, of the amount of the profits or losses on Friday of each week, and in the absence of such notice, the Yield will be deemed to have been earned. If the Yield is not earned in any week, the Investor may call for immediate repayment of the Funds and any accrued and unpaid Yield. The Manager agrees that any claim for loss of any part of the Funds may only be proved by the testimony of two witnesses admissible in accordance with the strictest Orthodox Jewish law before a duly constituted Orthodox Rabbinical Court comprising such rabbis as the Investor may designate in good faith. The Manager agrees that any claim of failure to achieve the Yield shall be binding on the Investor only if the absolute precise amount is proved by an oath of the Manager pursuant to the provision of the strictest Orthodox Jewish law. Such oath shall be of the most onerous of the many forms of oath provided by Orthodox Jewish law, to be taken by the Manager during the course of the reading of the Torah, in such Orthodox Synagogue as may be designated by the Investor, and in the attendance of the Rabbi, the full congregation then in attendance, and a valid Orthodox Rabbinical Court. Failing proof of aforesaid as to the loss of Funds or failure to achieve the Yield, the Funds and the Yield shall be deemed owing as and when due, as set out herein, and the Manager shall be obligated to pay such amounts. Any unpaid portion of the Funds or the Yield shall be deemed reinvested in accordance with the terms of this *heter iska*, both before and after the Maturity Date. This document shall supersede the provisions of any other agreement between the parties which may be inconsistent with this *heter iska*. However, if a Mortgage or other security ("the Security") has been provided by the Manager to the Investor, it shall serve to secure the Manager's obligations hereunder, and the rights and remedies set out in and arising under the Security may be enforced by the Investor in such manner as provided for it in the event of a default by the Manager, subject only to the Manager's right to prove loss of Funds or failure to achieve the Yield, in the manner set out above.

Dated and signed this _________ day of _______ , _______ (year),

in the city of _______________ .

Investor _________________________   Manager _________________________

From *A Matter of Interest,* by Rabbi Mordechai Kanner, Targum Press, 2002. Reprinted with permission from the author

STUDENT RESOURCE 21

PAYMENT METHODS

CASH

PROS

- People know whether they have money to spend.
- The money is tangible, not an abstract number on a bank or credit card statement. This creates greater psychological resistance to parting with it, and leads people to think more about spending it.
- From the standpoint of financial responsibility and restraint, many of the disadvantages of cash are actually advantages.

CONS

- People often don't have cash readily available, and obtaining cash can be a hassle.
- Obtaining cash may involve bank fees.
- There is no recourse in the event of loss or theft.
- Once payment is made, the money cannot be retrieved. (Unlike a check or credit card payment that can be stopped.)
- Payment has to be made in person; it cannot be made by telephone, by mail or online.
- Cash transactions are difficult to track or keep records of.
- Possibility of counterfeit bills.

CHECK

PROS

- Payment can be made by mail.
- Can be used when there is no cash available.
- Can be post-dated to delay payment.
- Can be stopped in the event of loss, theft, or a payment dispute.
- Convenient as a deposit on a purchase or as a form of guarantee.
- Payment can be made in advance, on any date in the future.

CONS

- Check payments are difficult to track because it is uncertain when the checks will be deposited.
- When more than one person is writing checks on an account, it can lead to chaos.
- Bounced checks, or checks that have mistakes or other technical problems can lead to inconvenience, embarrassment and hefty charges.
- Possibility of fraud.
- Ease of delaying payment may cause people to go into debt.

CREDIT CARD

PROS

- Convenient and available.
- Insurance against theft.
- Easy to cancel in the event of loss.
- Payment can be made by telephone or online.
- Can be used anywhere in the world.
- Can be used by all members of the family.
- Easy to track.
- Credit limits make it impossible to spend more than a certain amount.
- Payment can be made in installments.
- Earn air miles and rewards.

CONS

- People spend more (30% more, studies show) because it is convenient and because they do not feel the pain of parting with their money.
- Multiple credit cards can lead to chaos.
- Paying in installments can lead to exceeding budgetary limits.
- Credit option can be halachically problematic.
- Credit cards deceive people into thinking that they have money when they really do not.
- Incurs high interest if paid late.

STUDENT RESOURCE 22

DR. SEUSS ON Consumerism

Consumerism is based on creating needs where none existed before.

In **The Lorax**, by Dr. Seuss, a fellow opens a factory for a new type of garment called a "Thneed," and a creature named the Lorax ridicules him for creating this useless item. To which the fellow responds:

"A Thneed's a fine something that all people need!
It's a shirt. It's a sock. It's a glove. It's a hat.
But it has other uses. Yes, far beyond that.
You can use it for carpets. For pillows! For sheets!
Or curtains! Or covers for bicycle seats!"

The Lorax said, "Sir! You are crazy with greed.
There is no one on earth
who would buy that fool Thneed!"
But the very next minute I proved he was wrong.
For, just at that minute, a chap came along,
and he thought that the Thneed I had knitted was great.
He happily bought it for three ninety-eight.

I laughed at the Lorax, "You poor stupid guy!
You never can tell what some people will buy."

STUDENT RESOURCE 23

AM I A SHOPAHOLIC?

Question: *Shopping has been my favorite pastime ever since I've been a teenager. I love to buy things – groceries, clothing, household items, you name it. I often find myself heading out to a store in the evenings when I have nothing else to do. I've noticed a pattern in which I'll go into a store on the spur of the moment and buy a few things, only to go back to that store a few days later to return some items, at which point I'll inevitably find something else to purchase. My family members and friends comment about my spending habits, calling me a "shopaholic" and telling me that I spend too much. How do I know if I really have a spending problem? And if I do have a spending problem, how can I overcome it?*

A: Not knowing the details of your lifestyle and spending habits, we cannot tell you whether you have a spending problem. But we can tell you that your willingness to confront the issue is a very good first step in overcoming your spending problem, if indeed you have one.

When does spending become a problem? Any type of behavior or characteristic taken to an extreme is problematic, and spending is no different. The Rambam teaches us that the middle road is the golden path, and the ability to strike a balance between the two extremes in every middah is the hallmark of healthy behavior.

Spending problems come in two varieties – stinginess and extravagance, representing the two polar extremes of the spending spectrum. Our goal is to find a middle road that allows us to spend enough to meet our needs and obligations, but not so much that we squander money needlessly.

The terms "stinginess" and "extravagance" are quite subjective, because the size of a person's budget is a major factor in determining whether the person spends too much or too little. But how much money a person has is by no means the only factor in determining whether he or she has a spending problem. Spending problems are as a much a behavioral issue as a financial issue. There are poor people who are miserly, and there are rich people who are miserly. There are poor people who overspend, and there are rich people who overspend.

The sign of a stinginess problem is when a person has difficulty spending money on items that he and his family clearly require – not because he doesn't have the money, but because he cannot bring himself to spend it. This creates an atmosphere of deprivation and penny-

Reprinted from *Your Money and Your Life: Mesila's Down-to-Earth, Torah-Based Strategies for Managing Your Finances*, by M. Heimowitz

pinching in the home, which is often accompanied by a fixation with money and prices.

When does overspending become a problem? For every person, the line between healthy spending and overspending will be drawn in a different place, but we can identify four general parameters that can help you to determine whether you are overspending.

1. **You spend more than you can afford.** There are three ways to assess whether you are spending more than you can afford. One, if you consistently spend more than you earn, and you either accumulate debt or eat away at your savings as a result. Two, if your income is reasonable but you are nevertheless unable to put aside any money for the future. And three, if you spend money on luxury or non-essential items and you are then unable to pay for basic or essential items.

2. **You spend money to fill an emotional void.** While shopping can be a pleasurable experience and can provide some measure of stress relief, it should not be used consistently as an outlet for negative feelings such as sadness, inadequacy, boredom, guilt, fear, anger, or nervousness. Spending money is not a healthy response to negative feelings, because the act of swiping a credit card and walking away with a shopping bag does nothing to dispel the source of those feelings. Any feeling of emotional relief that shopping provides is therefore short-lived and superficial.

3. **You buy things that you do not need and never use.** If your closet is full of items that still have price tags, if you often wonder what possessed you to buy a particular item that you have no use for, or if you frequently make excuses for – or worse, lie about – your purchases and how much they cost, then it is likely that your spending is problematic.

4. **Your spending is adversely affecting other areas of your life.** Even if you and your family are not suffering financially because of your spending habits, your spending might be harmful to you or to your loved ones in other ways. Do you have frequent arguments with your family members about your spending habits? Are your children being neglected because you are out shopping too much? Has your marriage been reduced to a collection of shared things, instead of shared goals and shared communication? Does your life revolve around material acquisition, to the point that you are desensitized to the pleasures of spirituality and meaningful relationships?

Severe Overspending

In extreme cases, people can actually develop an addiction to shopping – known scientifically as oniomania, or colloquially as "shopaholism" – if they get used to spending money in order to squelch negative feelings. These people might buy ten items when they really need only one, or they might pay outrageous amounts of money for things they have little or no use for.

Shopping addicts experience a rush of endorphins when they spend money, which gives them a brief but exhilarating escape from life's painful realities. As soon as that feeling of euphoria subsides, they begin to crave the pleasurable sensation they associate with shopping, and they feel an uncontrollable urge to spend money again. Between spending episodes, shopping addicts are typically plagued by anxiety, shame, and guilt, and think about money excessively. This cycle is typical of addictive behavior, and professional intervention is usually required in order to break the cycle.

Overcoming the Problem

If your spending has reached out-of-control proportions, to the point where it can be classified as compulsive or addictive, then you will need to seek professional help. But if you still have some measure of control over your spending, we will offer several suggestions for reining it in to a point where it is no longer problematic.

› Don't carry your wallet with you when you don't need it. If you don't have money or a credit card with you, then you will have to come back later if you want to buy an item that you see. This is a good way to test whether you really need or want the item, and can help to reduce impulse purchases.

› Get rid of your credit cards. When used properly, credit cards can be a very convenient and useful tool. But if you have a tendency to overspend, you should avoid credit cards completely. Credit cards make it dangerously easy to spend money, since they eliminate the pain you experience when you have to part with your money. The pain of parting with money is actually a healthy pain, because it ensures that you item you are spending money on justifies the pain involved.

› Shop when you are not sad, stressed, excited, or in a rush. People tend to spend more, and buy things they don't need, when they are feeling down, or when they are under pressure. People who are very happy, excited, or on an emotional high also tend to spend more. And the less time people have, the more money they tend to spend.

› Avoid temptation. Stay away from the stores you tend to spend money in. If you have a particular friend who spends a lot, don't go shopping with her.

› Develop constructive emotional outlets. There are many constructive ways to relieve negative feelings, but spending money is not one of them. If you are feeling down, talk to a friend, pick up a Tehillim, or go for a walk, instead of heading instinctively for the mall. Keep in mind that "retail therapy" is therapeutic for retailers, not for customers.

› Find alternative recreational activities. You don't have to buy anything in order to have a good time. Instead of associating shopping with leisure and relaxation, condition yourself to see shopping primarily as a functional and task-oriented activity, and plan leisure activities that do not involve any purchases.

› Learn to express love and gratitude in non-tangible ways. People who enjoy buying things often ascribe disproportionate value or importance to tangible objects and resort to gift-giving in order to express love and gratitude. But emotions like these are best expressed in words, whether spoken or written. Tangible gifts should be reserved for special occasions; otherwise, they lose their value in the eye of the recipient. Even when you do decide to buy a gift, remember that a gift is only as meaningful as the sentiment underlying it, and the amount of money you spend on a gift does not determine its value.

› Build a budget that includes an allowance for discretionary spending. If you tend to overspend, then it is doubly important for you to have a clearly defined budget that governs the amount you spend on variable expenditures such as food, clothing, gifts, and household items. But in order for you to succeed in sticking to your budget, it is also important that you give yourself some breathing room and allocate some money towards non-essential or impulse purchases. This way, you will not feel stifled by your budget and you will not be tempted to abandon it any time you succumb to the temptation to buy something that is not absolutely necessary. To make sure that you remain accountable to your budget, you should build it together with your spouse or a close friend or relative, and review it together with that person on a regular basis.

We welcome readers' suggestions for other ways to kick the overspending habit, and we wish you much success.

STUDENT RESOURCE 24

CLIMBING THE MOUNTAIN OF CREDIT CARD DEBT

Question: *I know that Mesila is against using credit cards, but I have found that it is difficult for me to keep the right amounts of cash on hand, and I often resort to using my credit card. As a result, I've built up a bit of a balance on my credit card – or cards, I should say – and I'm wondering if you have any advice how I can pay it off.*

A: Mesila is not, in principle, opposed to credit cards, nor do we consider cash the preferred payment method in all situations. One of Mesila's guiding principles is to promote financial management principles and attitudes that are universally relevant, while avoiding specific tips and suggestions. So rather than issuing a blanket statement regarding whether you should be using credit cards or not, we will share several general guidelines that should help you decide for yourself.

Credit cards can be a very useful and convenient tool, when used correctly. The trouble is that many people misuse their credit cards by charging more than they can afford each month. Credit card companies actually *rely* on people misusing their cards; in fact, interest charged on outstanding balances represents the primary way in which credit card companies generate revenue. In 2007, people in the U.S. who carried a monthly balance paid $18.1 billion in penalty fees. With annual earnings of about $30 billion, the credit card industry is the most profitable one in the United States.

There are many advantages to using credit cards. You never run of out money. You are generally insured against theft, and you can easily cancel the card if you lose it. In contrast, cash that is lost or stolen is usually gone forever. You can use your credit card to pay for purchases by telephone or online, rather than mailing a check or paying by cash in person. Most credit cards can be used anywhere in the world, regardless of the local currency, and you can order cards for all of your family members. Depending on the card issuer's policy, purchases made using the card may be protected against theft, loss, or accidental damage that occurs within a certain period of time.

Credit card statements make it relatively straightforward to track your purchases on a monthly basis and keep a record of how your money is being spent. Cash, on the other hand, has no paper trail, and it is difficult to remember exactly where the money in your wallet went.

We will point out that all of these advantages are available through bank or debit cards as well, although purchase protection may not be offered on certain debit cards. The big difference, however, is that these cards draw on money that is already in your bank account, rather than creating a de facto debt that has to be paid at the end of the billing cycle. The only feature that credit cards offer that debit cards do not usually have is the possibility of earning rewards, in the form of airline miles, cash-back offers, or other perks.

So much for the advantages of using credit cards. Now let's talk about the drawbacks. Drawback number one is that they make it deceptively easy to spend money, whether you have the money or you don't. The act of swiping a credit card is not nearly as painful as taking actual money out of your wallet, and the psychological deterrent to parting with your money is therefore lessened considerably when paying with a credit card. Studies show that people spend about 30% more when paying by credit card than when paying with cash, and we think it is fair to assume that the extra 30% is money that could have been put to better use.

The other major drawback of credit cards is that they are a form of loan. When you take a loan, you borrow money and commit to repaying it at a later date. When you use a credit card, you also borrow money – but without realizing it. Mesila's philosophy is that a loan in which you realize that you are borrowing money is preferable to a loan in which you do not realize that you are borrowing money, simply because you are less likely to borrow, and more likely to repay, when the decision to take the loan was a conscious one.

Credit card debt is one of the worst forms of debt, for two reasons. One, it usually carries very high interest rates. Two, there is no repayment deadline for the debt. As long as you keep making minimum payments, credit card companies are quite happy to keep tacking interest onto your balance and let your debt swell to ever-greater proportions. Unpleasant as it may be to have creditors breathing down your back, it is a far healthier situation when a debt is collected at the end of its term than when a debt is allowed to balloon endlessly.

Not only do credit cards charge high interest rates, but there is very little limit as to how much they can raise your rate. Credit card companies are legally allowed to monitor your credit report, and should you make a late payment on a loan, a different credit card, or a utility bill, your interest rates can be increased dramatically, even if you have never missed a payment on that particular card.

There are a number of other reasons you may see your rates spike. These include bouncing a check, exceeding your credit limit, having too much debt or credit, getting a new credit card, and applying for an auto loan or mortgage.

Because credit card debt is so dangerous, our advice is that the only people who should use credit cards are those who (a) can rein in their spending despite the painless convenience of plastic and (b) pay their balance in full every month consistently. People who swipe their cards without giving it the same thought that they would when spending cash should rather spend cash, unless they are paying for something that they cannot possibly be spending more for by using a credit card (dental work, for instance, or a utility bill). And people who carry over a balance on their credit cards, even occasionally, should probably avoid using credit cards completely.

If you are able to use a credit card correctly, there are a few things we recommend:

› *Choose the right card.*

Make sure that your card provides a grace period of at least 20 days from the date of purchase until payment is due. Without a grace period, you'll be charged interest before you even get your bill. There are cards that offer airline miles, cash back on purchases, and points for rewards programs, and if you are using a credit card, you might as well get something in return. However, if there is an annual fee associated with your rewards card, make sure the benefits outweigh the cost.

› *Don't have too many cards.*

Keeping track of even one credit card can be quite a challenge. When keeping track of two or more cards, mistakes (such as missed payments or forgetting to cancel the card before annual fees kick in) are more likely to go by unnoticed. Unless you have a very good reason for keeping a second or third credit card, get rid of it.

But what if you have already fallen into credit card debt? Here are some suggestions for climbing out of the morass.

› *Ask for clemency.*

If you missed only one payment, you can call your credit card company and ask them to waive interest and late fees. Credit card companies will waive these fees on occasion, if you generally pay on time.

› *Stop using your credit cards.*

If you're already behind on your monthly payments, don't aggravate the situation by accumulating more credit card debt. Although this may seem obvious, it is actually the opposite of how people generally work. The tendency is that once people owe money, they lose a major psychological deterrent towards borrowing, and they let their debt slowly inflate. ("What's the difference if I owe $600 or $900?" "If I already owe $60,000, another $5,000 won't make any difference.") Cut your losses *now*, and don't allow yourself to charge even one additional item.

› *Take out a loan to pay off your credit card debt.*

Almost any type of loan is preferable to credit card debt because interest rates are generally much lower and there is a specific repayment timeframe. With a loan, you can work out repayment terms that reflect your ability to repay, which helps you discipline yourself to put aside a fixed sum every month for debt repayment. With credit card debt, there is no such discipline, since there is no obligation to repay anything more than the minimum payment.

› *Do a balance transfer to another card.*

While you will pay a fee, transferring your outstanding balance to a card with a lower interest rate will decrease the amount you carry from month to month. By doing a balance transfer instead of allowing interest fees to build up, you give yourself some breathing room to pay off your debt. But beware – this is a very stopgap measure. You can't keep doing balance transfers for very long since there are only so many transfers credit card companies will allow you to do, and besides, multiple balance transfers will cause your finances to become chaotic.

› *Find a card with a low interest rate.*

Some credit cards offer relatively low interest rates. Shopping around for a better rate than the one you currently have can save you hundreds or even thousands of dollars a month (that is, if your credit rating is good enough for you to be eligible for these offers). Look out, however, for introductory offers that end after several months or exclusions that limit the low rate to new purchases only.

› *Negotiate a better interest rate.*

You might have to spend a long time on the phone with your credit card company, but it's worth it to get your interest rate reduced by even a few points. If possible, ask your company to match another company's offer. If your company is unwilling to cooperate, you can mention that you may be forced to declare personal bankruptcy, if that is really an option. This gets the companies scared, because they are the ones who stand to lose from a bankruptcy.

› *Never, ever miss a minimum payment.*

Missing minimum payments is a big no-no, and can severely damage your credit rating. Having a good credit rating is important, because many types of creditors besides credit card companies – including utilities, hospitals, landlords, insurance companies, and banks – can report delinquent payments to credit bureaus, as well as access your credit history. Since credit card companies are among those monitoring and contributing to customers' credit reports, a late or missed payment on one charge account could cause your rates and fees to increase on a completely separate account – even your car insurance premiums.

Pay off credit card balances from smallest to largest.

The smallest debts are the easiest to pay off, and clearing them out of the way helps you make the fastest progress towards getting your finances in order. The fewer debts you have to pay back, the easier it will be to see the light at the end of the tunnel, and the more motivated you will be to tackle the larger, scarier debts.

› ***Make micro-payments.***

In addition to the minimum payments, send in whatever small amounts you can to gradually pay off your balance.

› ***Get professional debt counseling assistance.***

Climbing a mountain of credit card debt can be a very tough task to tackle alone. If there is a Mesila branch in your community, we encourage you to apply for our family coaching program. If there is no Mesila branch in your community, seek the guidance of a qualified debt coach.

STUDENT RESOURCE 25

MORTGAGE PAYMENTS & INTEREST

(IN-CLASS EXERCISE)

A. Comparative Table

	30-year mortgage 7% interest	30-year mortgage 4.5% interest	15-year mortgage 7% interest	15-year mortgage 4.5% interest	30-year mortgage 4.5% interest
Loan amount	$200,000	$200,000	$200,000	$200,000	$300,000
Annual interest rate	7%	4.5%	7%	4.5%	4.5%
Loan period in years	30	30	15	15	30
Monthly payment	$1,330.60	$1,013.37	$1,797.66	$1,529.99	$1,520.06
Number of payments	360	360	180	180	180
Total interest owed	$279,017.80	$164,813.42	$123,578.18	$75,397.58	$247,220.13
Total money paid (principal + interest)					

B. Questions

1. What are the advantages of a 30-year-loan over a 15-year?
2. What are the advantages of a 15-year-loan over 30-year?
3. In the last row of the above table, fill in the actual amounts repaid over the term of the loan in each of the four scenarios.
4. Abe and Debbie Halevi have four children, the oldest of whom is an eight-year-old boy. They need a $200,000 mortgage to buy a house, and interest rates are at 4.5%. They can comfortably afford to pay $1200 a month for their mortgage, but paying $1500 a month would be a strain on their budget, and would require them to tighten their belts significantly. What considerations should they take into account when deciding between a 15-year mortgage and a 30-year?

   - **Inflation** – money is worth less over time, so $1500 gets easier to pay over time.
   - **Weddings** – in 15 years, the Halevi's will likely have children getting married, and they will probably prefer not to have to be paying a mortgage then.
   - **Higher expenses** – as children grow older and the family grows, cost of living increases dramatically.
   - **Higher income** – as people grow older and become more experienced and established in their fields, their income generally increases.

5. Abe and Debbie decide to stretch themselves to pay $1500/month for a 15-year mortgage. Then, they realize that their car is getting old, and their new house can use some renovations. Of course, they also need furniture. Their mortgage broker offers them a $300,000, 30-year mortgage for practically the same monthly payment as the $200,000, 15-year. If you were in their shoes, what would you do? Why?

STUDENT RESOURCE 26

TAKING CHARITY ON A ONE-TIME BASIS

Question: *I work as a sofer, and I earn a modest income that is usually enough to cover my family's needs on a month-by-month basis. I have never earned much money, but I also never thought of myself as "poor." Several months ago, I injured my wrist, and I was sidelined from work for about a month. During that period, I had no choice but to borrow money from a gemach and from a couple of friends in order to live. Now, I am baruch Hashem able to work again, but I am left with a considerable amount of debt that I do not see how I can repay. A local tzedakah organization is aware of my financial plight, and they offered me a one-time grant to pay off my debts and put me back onto my feet.*

To me, taking tzedakah is anathema, and I would like to avoid it at all costs. But I honestly don't really see any option at this point. I am considering applying for Mesila's services, but because you do not give people tzedakah, I am not sure that you can help me. Is there anything Mesila can do for me?

A: You are to be commended for your reluctance to take tzedakah money. Jews have always gone to great lengths to avoid taking alms, and for good reason. The Talmud (*Beitzah* 32b) says about a person who depends on others for sustenance that the world is dark for him, and that his life is not life. Obviously, taking tzedakah money is something that the Torah views as a last resort, and something that should be avoided if at all possible.

Lehavdil, in the world of economics, evidence abounds that welfare programs actually increase dependency and perpetuate poverty. When people get money for doing nothing, they invariably lose some of their motivation to work for money. This is a psychological reality that is difficult to overcome.

If you were to accept tzedakah, even if only on a one-time basis, you will have crossed the line from financial independence to dependency. And once you cross that line, it will become far more difficult for you to refrain from accepting tzedakah again.

You write that Mesila does not give people tzedakah. It is true that in most cases we do not give out tzedakah *money*, but we actually do give people tzedakah. The highest form of tzedakah, according to the Rambam and the *Shulchan Aruch*, is helping a person become self-sufficient and not need to take money from others. The counseling services we provide put people on their feet while preserving their dignity and financial independence.

In Mesila's ten years of working with families experiencing financial difficulties – and these, by the way, are not limited to "poor" families – we have found that money is not necessarily the solution to financial problems. Financial problems are usually the result of lack of knowledge and poor financial management skills. By helping people to acquire the necessary knowledge and financial management skills, Mesila has helped hundreds of families and businesses to solve their financial problems.

The fact that some tzedakah organizations today are beginning to offer Mesila-style counseling services is an indication that more and more people are realizing that very often, money alone will not solve financial problems. In your case specifically, taking tzedakah on a one-time basis might cover your shortfall for the time being, but it will not prevent a similar crisis from recurring in the future. It also establishes a dangerous precedent.

Let's face it: living from month to month leaves you little financial breathing room, and you could easily land up in debt again in the future. This is not a pessimistic view of your situation; it is a realistic assessment.

If there is a Mesila branch in your community, we encourage you to apply for our counseling services. Mesila can help you develop a budget that will allow you to cover your living expenses, pay off your debts (slowly, if necessary), and save up money for unforeseen expenses or "rainy day" situations such as an injured wrist. (Mesila includes unforeseen expenses in the category of foreseeable expenses. Smart budgeting always takes rainy days into account.)

A Mesila counselor can also help you find ways to increase your income and decrease your expenditures. This will give you the financial breathing room that will allow you to ride out minor financial crises that may arise in the future.

The Talmud (*Berachot* 5b) observes that "*Ein chavush matir atzmo mibeit ha'asurim*" – a prisoner cannot release himself from prison. When people are in the midst of difficult situations, they often are powerless to extricate themselves from their predicaments. This principle is extremely applicable to people going through financial difficulties. Even if you are a financially responsible person, you might find it extremely beneficial to have a resourceful, experienced, and objective Mesila coach tackling your financial issues together with you.

Before applying to Mesila, however, be aware that our counseling services are far-reaching and very thorough. Helping a family achieve financial stability is not something that can be accomplished overnight, and it takes months, and sometimes years, of counseling before the family becomes fully self-sufficient.

If there is no Mesila branch in your area, then we would recommend that you take the tzedakah offered to you, but that you try to view it as a loan, not as a handout. You can then slowly save up money to repay the "loan." When you save up enough money, you can make a donation to the organization that gave you the money. In this way, you can avoid the stigma of taking tzedakah.

If your local tzedakah organization offers any type of counseling, we strongly encourage you to accept it. These counseling services may not be as comprehensive or as structured as Mesila's, but they are certainly helpful nonetheless.

The Mishnah (*Pe'ah* 8:9) says that if a person needs tzedakah but refrains from taking it, he will eventually be able to support others with his own money. Although this mishnah does not apply to someone who is unable to survive without taking tzedakah, we believe that in your case it probably does apply. If you can find a way out to avoid taking tzedakah, you will reap the benefits of remaining financially independent in both this world and the next.

Part 3:

Assignments

To be used with Unit 1

Assignment #1:
Priorities and Spending Attitudes

Objective:

To examine the differing needs and wants among people from different generations, societies, or backgrounds.

Instructions:

1. Choose two interviewees who come from different backgrounds. (Note: The more different your interviewees, the easier this assignment will be for you.)
2. Develop interview questions (8-10) pertaining to spending attitudes and habits, as well as their decision-making process in their purchases. You may use some or all of the sample questions below, but you must also develop some of your own.
   a. What do you consider a need that others might consider a want? What luxuries can you live without that others might consider a necessity?
   b. How did the society you grew up in shape your personal needs and wants?
   c. What did you lack growing up that you wish until this day that you had had? What did you lack growing up that you feel made you into a better person?
   d. Was there ever a time that you lacked something that you absolutely needed? How did you manage?
   e. What's the biggest mistake you think people make when it comes to spending money?
   f. Can you think of a time that you decided not to buy something even though you had the money for it and it was something you could have used?
   g. What do you think is the best advice a parent can give their child about spending?

3. Write an essay (2-3 pages) on one of the following topics.

a. **Topic #1:** Compare and contrast the answers of your two interviewees. How did their differing backgrounds impact their spending and decision-making habits?

b. **Topic #2:** "Our luxuries become our children's necessities." Explain this statement, and state whether you agree or disagree with it, using examples from your two interviewees.

To be used with Unit 2

Assignment #2:
Creating a Business Plan

Objective:

To learn how to develop a rudimentary business plan.

Planning is an essential step in earning and enhancing your income. In this assignment, you will develop a plan for starting a new business.

Directions:

Develop an idea for a new business in your community that you think would be profitable. Then, write a plan for taking your business idea from concept to reality, using the questions in the following sections as a guide. Each section should be clearly labeled with the appropriate section name and written in paragraph format (1-3 paragraphs per section).

Note: Not every question will be relevant to every type of business. You may choose to address a minimum of 5 out of the following 10 sections.

1. **Products & Services:** List all of your major products or services. What benefits will they bring your customers? What needs are you filling?
2. **Customers:** Who are your potential customers? For each customer group, construct what is called a demographic profile, including characteristics such as: age, gender, location, income level, education, and industry-specific factors.
3. **Competition:** Who are your direct competitors? What are their strengths and weaknesses (prices, location, service etc.) compared to you (go & visit them!)?
4. **Differentiation:** What is special or unique about what you are offering? What is your niche, your unique corner of the market? What differentiates you from your competitors? Why should customers buy your products or services rather than those of your competitors?
5. **Distribution:** How do you plan to distribute your products or services? Will you sell directly to the customers or sell through agents or retailers (stores) etc.?

6. **Marketing & Promotion:** How will your customers know about you? Which media will you use for advertising, and why specifically those? What image do you want to project? How do you want customers to see you? What's your busy season? Your dry season? How will you weather the dry seasons? What marketing strategies can you employ to drum up business during the dry spells?

7. **Location:** What is the ideal location for your business? Take into account financial realities (prime real estate is expensive) as well as your need for visibility to your customers. (A pizza shop or clothing has to be located on a main street to attract walk-in traffic; a travel agency or shipping company does not.)

8. **Management:** Which skills and personality traits do you possess that make you qualified to start and manage this business? Which aspects of this business will you find challenging, considering your unique personality and skill set? What education or training will you need to get your business started?

9. **Personnel:** What type of employees will you need and for which functions? Which responsibilities will you handle yourself and which responsibilities will you delegate to employees? (e.g., sales, bookkeeping, maintenance, secretarial duties, etc.)?

10. **Halachic & Ethical Issues:** What halachic or ethical issues do you anticipate arising in the planning or running of your business? How will you deal with these issues?

11.* **Financial:** (Note: This section is more technical and complex than the others and should be used or omitted at the teacher's discretion. Before assigning this section, all terms should be explained and the relevant calculations demonstrated.)

   a. Investment budget: How much money will you need to start up your business? This figure should include all your startup costs (such as licenses, equipment, inventory, etc.) plus operating costs for your first three months. How will you finance these initial costs?

   b. Profit & loss budget: How much of your product or service will you have to sell each month in order to cover costs? (This is known as your "break-even point.") In order to calculate this, answer the following questions:

      How much will the product cost you to produce or purchase? How much will you be selling it for? What is your profit margin (selling price minus cost to produce or purchase)? What fixed costs (known as overhead) will you have (electricity, rent, etc.)?

   c. Cash flow budget: How much money do you foresee coming in (revenues) and how much money do foresee going out (payments) during the first three months of your business?

To be used with Unit 3

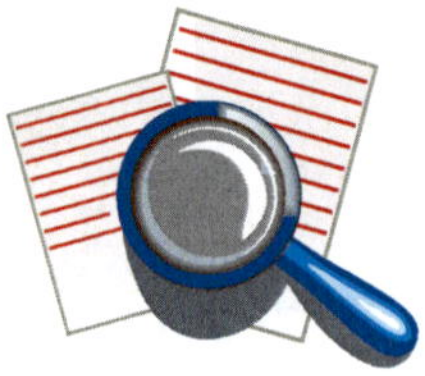

Assignment #3:
Summer Camp Budget

Objective:

To research the costs associated with summer camp and develop a comprehensive yet reasonable summer budget for a camper.

Directions:

Going to summer camp can entail many expenses, both before and during the camp season.

1. Camp fees: How much does the camp charge for one month?
2. Shopping for camp: What items will the camper need to buy before camp starts? How many of each item? Be as specific as possible (for example, write "sleeping bag, mosquito repellant, flashlight," rather than "camping gear"). How much will each of these items cost?
3. Camp expenses: Which expenses will there be while the camper is at camp? How much will each of these expenses be?
4. What is the total amount the camper will require in order to meet all of the above expenses comfortably?
5. Suggest four ways to bring down the cost of camp significantly without severely compromising the summer experience. Your suggestions should relate to each of the three expense categories discussed in questions 1-3. (For example: Are the camp fees flexible?)
6. Which of the changes you suggested will be easiest to implement? Which will be the most difficult? Why?
7. How does your camping budget incorporate the rule of "Everything you need and some of what you want"? Give specific examples.
8. Using Mesila's budgeting forms as a guide (see the Mesila Student Guide to Budgeting), create a budget table of camp expenses for your camper.

To be used with Unit 3

Assignment #4:
Banking Procedures & Services

Objective:

In chart form, compare the banking procedures and services of two banks.

Directions:

Choose two types of accounts (checking/ savings/ CDs) and compare at least three procedures and services offered, and the fees incurred (transfer/ reporting/ receive alerts/ place stop payment / etc.). Create a chart for each bank of your choice.

For example:

City Bank

	Checking Account	Savings Account	Certificate of Deposit
Transfer funds - Possible?			
Transfer funds - Fee?			
Monthly reports - Possible?			
Monthly reports - Fee?			
Receive alerts - Possible?			
Receive alerts - Fee?			

To be used with Unit 4

Assignment #5:
You be the Financial Advisor

Mesila's Common Sense Rules for Investors

1. If something sounds too good to be true, it probably is.
2. People who try to get rich quick often lose a lot of money quick.
3. If someone is pressuring you to invest and telling you that the opportunity can't wait, you'd better wait.
4. High returns = high risk. The more money you stand to make, the more money you stand to lose. (If the risks would be low, they wouldn't have to offer such high returns in order to entice people to invest with them.)
5. Bank investments (savings accounts, CDs, etc.) are considered risk-free. Any investment that pays higher returns than the bank is not risk free. But without any risk, you cannot earn more than the bank offers.
6. For every person, there is an appropriate level of risk, depending on how much they can afford to lose. You can take risks only if you are prepared and able to deal with the worst-case scenario (which might mean losing your entire investment, part of it, or having your money tied up for an extended period).
7. "Buy the rumor, sell the news": A hot stock tip that's already public knowledge or is being advertised in the paper is not likely to bring any meaningful returns.
8. Sometimes, a seemingly good investment may be overpriced, which means that you are unlikely to realize any significant returns. A good investment is one that is worth the money you are investing; a bad investment is one for which you overpay.
9. Investments that are based on loopholes or wheeler-dealer schemes are usually not stable investments. Stable investments generally provide some product or service that advances people's needs in some way.
10. Good businessmen and seasoned investors do not need students (or the like) to recruit capital for them, and solid investment opportunities are usually snapped up long before they reach the doors of a school. The types of business deals and

investment opportunities that make it through the doors of yeshivos are often the types that are suited to gullible people only.

11. You have more to lose when investing with a friend or relative than with a stranger. With a stranger, all you can lose is money – with a friend, you can lose a friendship as well.
12. Before investing, do your due diligence. That means carefully investigating the opportunity and consulting with professionals and financial advisors regarding the particular opportunity so that you fully understand the risks involved and are equipped to make informed decisions.

This is a situation that a fellow named Simon presented to Mesila (details have been changed):

Morris, an old friend of mine, recently approached me with a very exciting investment opportunity. Morris's father owns an apartment building that is currently being rented to low-income tenants. He wants to renovate the apartments so that he can rent them out to higher-income tenants for double the rent. "Whatever money you invest with my father will triple in under five years," Morris promises. "But you need to hurry! The bank approved financing for this project, but my father needs investors to sign up within 48 hours – otherwise, the financing will fall through."

When I asked Morris whether the plan had any possible risks, he looked hurt. "This is a foolproof plan," he assured me. "Anyone with a little business sense would understand that in a minute. We just need to make sure that we can get rid of all the old tenants and get the building back up to 95% occupancy within six months. But that should be a cinch."

I know Morris well, and he is a reliable person and a capable businessman. Would you recommend that I invest with him?

Part 1.

Analyze the pros and cons of this investment opportunity. Think ahead. What difficulties may Morris and his father encounter with their plan? Does the plan involve any legal or ethical issues or potential pitfalls?

Part 2.

Referring to Mesila's Ten Common Sense Rules for Investors, which rules would Simon be following were he to invest with Morris? Which rules would he be breaking?

Part 3.

Using your answers to parts 1 & 2, write a response to Simon's query advising him whether to invest with Morris. (1-2 pages)

To be used with Unit 5

Assignment #6:
Making Informed Credit Card Choices

Assignment: You be the Financial Advisor

Getting a credit card offer in the mail can be exciting. Credit card companies think so, apparently – why else would they send out eight billion offers a year? (That's more than the number of people on the planet.)

But not all offers are created equal. Many people have fallen into the credit card trap and found themselves paying fees they never knew existed. That's why Senator Charles Schumer introduced into law a page of clearly stated disclosures and policies for every credit card. This "Schumer's Box" is now included in every credit card in the U.S.

Before signing up for your preapproved card, with fantastic miles programs and other perks, let's take a look at some different offers and see what makes some cards better than others.

Assignment:

1. Compare the disclosure box ("Schumer's box") of three different credit card offers.
2. What is your introductory interest rate on purchases (APR) and when does the introductory period expire?
3. What happens to your interest rate (APR) if you make one late payment?
4. Does the card have an annual fee? How much?
5. What is the interest rate on cash advances?
6. When does the company begin to charge interest on purchases? When does the company begin to charge interest on cash advances? If there is a difference, explain why it may be significant to the consumer.
7. Is there any circumstance under which the credit card company might change the interest rate?
8. What other factors make one card more attractive than the others?
9. Overall, which card do you recommend, and why?
10. In the absence of the Schumer's box, what information might the consumer have missed?

To be used with Unit 6

Assignment #7:
Home Ownership Considerations

Scenario

Dan and Jaclyn Barzilai are married eight years, with three children. They are currently renting a 3-bedroom apartment for $1200/month, and they would like to buy a house. The house that they're looking at is in passable condition, priced at $335,000, and is situated on the outskirts of a growing frum community.

Considerations

Location: Right now they are living right near their synagogues and schools and near the shopping and a great pizza store. The new house doesn't have such great neighbors…yet.

Repairs: The superintendent takes care of anything in the apartment that breaks. In the ramshackle "new" house, no one is sponsoring the repairs – and there are lots of repairs to be made.

Space: Three bedrooms, one bathroom with three kids is getting a little tight. The new house has four bedrooms, with an alcove that can be used as a study/playroom, an extra bathroom, a bigger living room/dining room and a semi-finished basement that "has potential." There is also a nice-sized backyard.

Financing: The bank will give them a mortgage of up to $235,000, which is 70% of the property value. They have an inheritance of $75,000 from their grandparents. They can borrow $25,000 from relatives and friends to complete the $100,000 down payment.

Payments: Presently, they are paying $1200 in rent. A 15-year mortgage of $235,000 at 5.5% interest will cost them $1900/month, and a 30-year mortgage at 6% (interest rates are usually higher on a longer-term mortgage) will cost them $1400/month. They can manage the 30-year mortgage on their current income, if they squeeze their budget. To be able to afford the 15-year mortgage, Dan and Jaclyn will have to find an additional source of income, but it will take only 15 years for the house to be theirs. They will also have to repay $500/month in private loans for the next four years, which will require them to pay a total of $1900 or $2400/month, depending which mortgage they take – a significant increase over the $1200 rent they are currently paying.

Possible Solution

Dan and Jaclyn decide to go for the 30-year mortgage, and put any extra money they have into their mortgage so that they can pay it off sooner. They can afford the $1400 mortgage, but they need money to pay off the private loans. They decide to buy the house and rent it out. Because the house is a little bit "out," they can get only about $1800/month in rent for it. If they can manage in their current location for another four years, the $1800 in rent will pay their own rent ($1200) plus their private loans ($500), with some allowance for repairs that their tenants will need ($100), while they pay an additional $1400/month for the mortgage. They are also hoping that they will be able to raise the rent on their house, as the neighborhood grows and their location becomes more desirable. Once the private loans are repaid, they can reevaluate.

Alternate Solution

The above solution is one of many possible solutions. Can you come up with an alternate solution to the Barzilai's housing dilemma? Address the above considerations (location, repairs, space, financing, payments) in your solution. Are there any other considerations you think they should take into account? (1 page)

To be used with Unit 7

Assignment #8:
Ethics in Personal Finance

Finances naturally raise many ethical challenges and dilemmas.
Describe and evaluate one such issue.

Directions:

Identify an issue in your community where the value of charity or financial integrity is being compromised. Pinpoint the underlying factors contributing to this issue. Explain and evaluate what is wrong and why it is wrong. How is the compromise of integrity being rationalized or justified? Suggest possible solutions that will rectify the ethical issue without causing damage to the people involved.

Submit answers in an essay format (2-3 pages).

To be used with Unit 7

Assignment #9:

Final Course Assignment
Personal Finance Portfolio & Reflection Exercise

Directions:

Part 1. Portfolio

Select the four written items you have prepared during this course that best exhibit your skills, achievements, and efforts within the course. Present this collection of your work as a portfolio showcasing what you have learned.

Part 2. Reflection and Evaluation Exercise

Describe in essay format (1-2 pages) what you have gained in this course. Use the questions below to guide your reflection (addressing at least four of the questions raised).

1. Which specific point raised in the course was most interesting or surprising to you? Why?
2. What part of this course was the least interesting or relevant to you? Why?
3. What are three things that you will do differently in your own financial life as a result of this class?
4. Which ideas covered in the course will be the hardest for you to implement? How do you intend to overcome those difficulties?
5. "Financial mismanagement can magnify or contribute to virtually any other problem."

   Explain this statement, giving specific examples to support it.
6. What personal finance advice or guidelines might you give to a friend based on what you have learned in this course? (Your advice should relate to a specific issue in personal finance, such as credit card use, taking loans, or career choices.)
7. How can the skills encouraged or strengthened in this course (such as prioritizing, decision-making, setting goals, accountability, resourcefulness, and delaying gratification) be applied to other areas of your life?
8. Have you shared anything you've learned in this class with parents, siblings or friends?

   Please elaborate.

Part 4:

The Mesila Student Guide to Budgeting

Table of Contents

A Note to the Student

Dear Student,

Life is not about money, but it sure gets messy when your finances are not in order or you can't live within your means. In theory, living within your means is very simple: spend less than you earn, and you'll be OK!

The problem is that we all have limited money at our disposal, yet there are unlimited possibilities as to what we can do with that money. So the challenge is to use our money in the way that will bring us the maximum benefit and cause us the least financial stress.

Facing this challenge successfully requires a proactive approach: namely, a budget plan. Most people don't like the word budget. It makes them break out into a sweat and think of lots of good reasons why now is not a good time to start budgeting, or why it's not necessary to have a budget.

The reason why budgeting seems so scary is because we tend to associate budgeting with restrictions, deprivation, and stress. People think, *If I have a budget, I'm not going to be able to buy what I want*, or, *If I start budgeting, I'm going to have to worry about how to make my finances work, and they just don't!*

But the truth is that budgeting is not about restrictions at all; it's about giving you **control** over your finances and **freedom** to use your money as you see fit. Your budget doesn't tell you how to spend your money – *you tell your budget how you want to spend your money*. Then your budget helps you to manage your finances in a way that will enable you to spend money on the things you really want.

You might be thinking: Why do I need to learn about this now? I don't have a budget! I don't have finances! I'm only in high school! But surprise, surprise! Now is the perfect time in your life to practice, precisely *because* you don't really have to be responsible for a family budget, which is a really complicated thing, and something that's tough to learn on the job.

Financial management is a very individual thing, and one that every family will approach differently. Nevertheless, having a budget is an important component of financial management **for everyone**. Some people's budgets are so detailed that they leave nothing to chance, and other people's budgets are only basic outlines, but every family needs to have some sort of budget plan in order to stay in – or get back into – the black. When we don't have a plan, we spend more than we can afford without even noticing, and we lose control over our wallets. But with a budget in hand, we regain control of our wallets. And that's a great feeling.

In this guide, you'll learn how to build an effective budget and cash flow plan, and how to avoid common budgeting pitfalls. To make budgeting as simple and straightforward as possible, the step-by-step instructions in the guide are written in clear, easy-to-understand language and are accompanied by frequently asked questions and section summaries.

If you're looking to strike it rich, this program is not for you. But if you're looking for a way to avoid the mistakes that others have made, and control your money instead of letting your money control you, then we hope you'll find this booklet helpful – now, and in the future *b'ezras Hashem*.

Mesila

The First Step: Establish Needs and Wants

Our goal in budgeting is to allow you to have *everything you need and some of what you want.* That means that you have to know the difference between what you need and what you want. It also means that you have to make sure FIRST that you have what you need, and only THEN see if you can have what you want.

Needs and wants are different for different people. Just because your friend, or your neighbor, or even your older sister *needs* something doesn't mean that you do. And just because they *don't need* something doesn't mean that you don't. That's why you have to get to know yourself, your needs, and your wants.

The purpose of the "Track What You Spend" exercise on the following page is:

1. To take note of spending habits so that we can get to know ourselves and how we spend.
2. To differentiate between needs and wants so that we can prioritize.

Other lessons to be learned from tracking what you spend:

1. For every outlay there must be a corresponding source of money. (Making that connection may be the most fundamental principle of financial stability.)
2. Becoming aware of your spending habits enables you to identify unhealthy patterns (or patterns that might become problematic later). **Awareness is the basis of all change.**

The Million Dollar Question

(Reprinted from Mirrors & Windows, by Malky Feig, with the permission of the Publisher. Mesorah Publications, 2005)

I was married two weeks
She, two months, an old pro.
We were discussing the financial issue,
two sages on the matter.
I said something
about newlyweds being stingy,
And she shook her head
waved her hand,
dismissed the idea.
"My husband says" –
she began importantly,
"There's no need to be stingy,
The golden rule is this:
You can buy whatever's necessary.
Just leave out the extras."
I was duly impressed
by her husband's wisdom.
Repeated the rule
to whomever was ready to listen.
I tried implementing it
in my own home,
Until I hit the catch –
The million-dollar question,
which I haven't quite figured out yet.
The rule is bliss,
It solves everything but this:
What are the necessities,
and what are the extras?

Track What You Spend!

Date: From__________ to __________

Purchase	Cost	Source of money	Need or Want?

Let's Get Honest.

(Discussion – in class, or with yourself)

1. How do you define "need"?
2. How do you define "want"?
3. Do the things you want bring you lasting benefit?
4. Which purchases do you regret a week later? Why do you have regrets?

Would a taxi ride to the other side of town (which costs more than a bus but saves an enormous amount of time) be a need or a want, especially when one is on a tight schedule?

Is a much needed vacation a "luxury"?

Does buying take out food when the Mom works full time constitute a need or want?

Should you buy your 13-year-old daughter a fancy camera that three quarters of the class has?

*When does a **want** become a **need**?*
There are no easy answers!

Let's Build a Family Budget

Here are some straightforward steps for creating a workable budget for a family. In other words: If you were trying to create a budget for your family – and b'ezras Hashem you will, one day – this is what you would do.

Step 1:

Determine the family's income

Start by adding up the family's net annual earnings, including:

- Monthly salary and wages (multiplied by twelve)
- Money from side jobs
- Investment earnings
- Interest and dividends
- Government allowances

If the family has any other sources of income (royalties, rent, parental support, etc.), include those as well.

A word of caution: Do not include possible windfalls – such as gifts or year-end bonuses – in your annual income projection.

If a person has bitachon (faith) that Hashem will provide for him, does he still have to budget?

Mesila actually posed this question to Hagaon R' Aaron Leib Steinman. R' Steinman replied, "If a person would go into a forest without water or food and then collapse, would that be *bitachon*? It would be suicide! Similarly, every person needs to live with a budget and calculate his income and expenses."

Budgeting and *bitachon* are not mutually exclusive. Even a person who has *bitachon* needs to budget, and even a person who budgets needs to have *bitachon*!

Let's Build a Family Budget (cont'd)

Step 2:

Track the family's expenses

To track expenses, write down every dollar the family spends for a minimum of 2-3 months. During this time, hold onto all documentation of the family's financial transactions, including:

- Bills
- Invoices
- Bank statements
- Credit card statements
- Cash register receipts

To keep track of expenses as they occur, keep a paper hanging in a conspicuous place – such as on the refrigerator – to remind you to record your expenses as they happen. Alternatively, you may want to carry a little notebook with you so that you can write down expenses as they occur. If you find it difficult to record expenses on an ongoing basis, you can take a few moments at the end of each day to record all of the day's expenses.

In addition to recording each purchase you make, you need to think about all of the other silent ways that money leaks out of your budget, such as:

- Bank and credit card charges
- Automatic bank account withdrawals
- Post-dated checks
- *Tzedakah* contributions
- Items you buy with pocket change

Pay attention to how often you spend small amounts – under $5. **These invisible or seemingly trivial expenses are often responsible for the discrepancy between what you think you spend and what you actually spend.**

Tracking your expenses might be difficult at first, but once you get used to doing it, it will become much easier – and you'll see the benefits very quickly! You'll be amazed at how your increased awareness will put you more in control of your money and help you make smarter spending decisions.

"Yikes! Where did all my money go?"

Has this ever happened to you? You take out your wallet, sure that it's going to be full – but it's empty! *Where did all the money go?* you wonder.

Keeping track of the small stuff is not only for your parents – it can do wonders for your own finances as well. Trivial purchases add up: $2 here, $5 here, and before you know it, that $100 your grandparents gave you is gone.

Try getting into the habit of jotting down what you spend so that you can gain control over your money and use your money in a way that you'll REALLY enjoy.

Should I be tracking all of my financial transactions on a regular basis?

At times, it is necessary to track financial transactions on a daily, item-by-item basis, such as when trying to create a budget and cash flow plan, or when faced with a large, one-time expense (such as a *simchah* or a home renovation). In addition, it is important to track all financial transactions for several months after implementing your budget and cash flow plan, until you are sure that you are successfully following the plan.

Even at other times, you still need to track your financial transactions on a general level to ensure that you are remaining within your budget. But it is not necessary to record every single transaction at that point; reviewing your bank and credit card statements and your check register should give you a pretty good picture of whether you are staying within budget.

If you find it liberating to record all of your financial transactions, since it gives you a sense of control over your money, then by all means, track every transaction. But if tracking your financial transactions down to the last penny makes you feel stifled, then do this detailed tracking only when absolutely necessary. The rest of the time, you can monitor your financial transactions on a more general level.

Step 3:
Calculate the family's expenses

After you have tracked the family's income and expenses for several months, you need to organize the data and group the different income and expense items into general categories. (For instance, group together related expenses such as "taxi ride," "bus card," and "train fare" under a general heading called "transportation.")

Expense categories can be divided into three major groups:

1. Fixed monthly expenses
2. Fluctuating monthly expenses
3. Annual or periodic expenses

Note: When calculating expenses, do not include debt payments (besides the mortgage).

Fixed monthly expenses may include things like:

- Mortgage or rent
- Insurance (life, health, home, auto, etc.)
- Car payments
- Childcare
- Savings plans
- Domestic help

There should be no need for guesswork here, since the amount you pay is usually the same every month.

Fluctuating monthly expenses are a bit trickier. Examples are:

- Food
- Utilities (telephone, cellular phone, electricity, water, gas, etc.)
- Gasoline
- Household products (toiletries, cleaning products, paper goods, etc.)
- Medications
- *Tzedakah* contributions
- Bank charges
- Dry cleaning

These expenses can vary significantly from month to month.

After tracking your expenses for 2-3 months, you should be able to determine a range for these fluctuating expenses. The numbers you will use in your budget should be the ones at the higher end of the range. For instance, if your food bill was $500 one month, $700 the next month, and $400 the next month, you might use $600 as a higher-end estimate of your monthly food costs.

All monthly expenses should be recorded under the month they were incurred, not the date they were paid. For example, if a pipe burst in your house on January 31 and you paid your plumber with a check dated February 28, record the cost of the repair under January's expenses.

Annual and periodic expenses are things like:

- Summer camp
- Medical and dental costs
- Clothing
- Shoes
- Vacations and outings
- *Smachot* and parties
- Home repairs
- Car maintenance
- Travel
- Chagim expenses
- Furniture and appliances

Estimate these costs to the best of your ability, using previous years' expenses as a guide.

To determine your total annual expenditure, add up your fixed and fluctuating monthly expenses and multiply the total by twelve. Then add to that your annual or periodic expenses.

Now that you have a fairly accurate estimate of your annual expenditure, pad this figure by 5-10% to allow room for unanticipated expenses. This will give your budget the flexibility to accommodate surprise expenses like parking tickets, lost knapsacks or passport renewals.

After you decide which items belong in which category, we recommend that you ask an objective person outside your immediate family – such as a friend, a neighbor, or a Mesila counselor – to review the items in each category and tell you whether your classifications seem reasonable. This will help you to discover any errors you have made, and may give you ideas for managing your money more effectively. Different families have different spending habits, and there is a lot you can learn a lot from comparing your family's spending habits with those of others.

Mesila's monthly and annual budgeting forms are designed to help you categorize your expenses in an orderly, logical fashion and show you where exactly your money is going.

Step 4:

Compare your income and expenses

Once you have determined how much you are actually spending on a monthly and annual basis, and you have tracked where all the money is going, you can measure your expenses against your income and determine your annual balance using the following formula:

Annual income – Annual expenses
= Annual balance

Now that you know what your annual balance is, you can congratulate yourself on having achieved financial awareness. **Awareness is the foundation for all improvement,** since you cannot fix something if you don't know what is wrong with it. If you and your spouse are aware of exactly what your financial situation is, you will be motivated to take the initiative to do whatever you can to improve it. Therefore, achieving awareness is the critical first step in gaining control of your finances, and is the basis for successful budgeting.

Why do I need to know what my annual balance is?

Your annual balance is *the* most important piece of budgetary information you have. Basically, it tells you whether your income exceeds your expenses, or the reverse.

If your annual balance is positive (which means that your income exceeds your expenses), that is the ideal situation: a surplus. You have extra money to save or use as you see fit, and you do not have the pressure of having to change your lifestyle. You may, however, choose to streamline your budget by "trimming the fat" and eliminating or reducing non-essential expenses. This will give you even more financial leverage and will allow you to put your money to the best possible use.

If your annual balance is negative (which means that your income is less than your expenses), you are running a deficit. Governments have the luxury of operating with a deficit; you do not. Even a small monthly deficit, when accumulated, can easily spiral into out-of-control debt. You therefore have to find additional sources of income and/or think of ways to cut down your expenses.

If your annual balance is zero (which means that your income and expenses are equal), then your budget is exactly balanced. Although on the surface, a perfectly balanced budget seems to be an acceptable situation, it is actually not acceptable, for several reasons:

1. It is almost impossible to calculate *all* of your expenses, so your expenses are probably 10-20% higher than you think. Therefore, if your budget is exactly balanced, you are probably running at least a small deficit.
2. A budget that is exactly balanced leaves you no leeway for unanticipated expenses – and there are *always* unanticipated expenses.
3. If your income and expenses are equal, then you have no possibility of saving for the future (or repaying debts, if you have any). Savings are an integral part of any budget, for they empower you to cope with financial challenges in the future and prevent those challenges from becoming crises. And it goes without saying that if you are in debt, it is critical that your budget be configured in a way that will enable you to repay your debts.

Step 5:

Build your budget plan

Now, you can go on to build a budget plan for the future, taking into account both your current income and spending information as well as future income and spending projections. How you will go about building your budget plans depends very much on whether your annual balance is positive or negative (an annual balance of zero is considered a negative balance, for our purposes).

When building your budget plan, it is critical to ensure that you have a significantly positive annual balance. If your annual balance is negative, or if you already have a positive annual balance but you wish to increase it, you will need to find ways to increase your income or reduce your expenses. The budget forms that you filled out earlier will play a vital role in helping you decide what budgetary changes to make.

Now, take a fresh set of monthly and annual budget forms and fill in projected future amounts for each item, based on the data you have collected and any budgetary changes you have decided to implement (i.e., increases in income and reductions in spending). Also include in your new budget any one-time earnings or expenses that you anticipate in the upcoming months. The projections you write down in this fresh set of forms will become your new budget plan.

Once you have successfully built a budget plan, you can go on to create a cash flow plan that will make your budget plan work for you.

Here are some general suggestions for **increasing income:**

- Learn new, marketable skills.
- Upgrade your professional abilities to make yourself more valuable to your employer and earn a promotion or raise.
- Turn a hobby into an income-generating activity.
- Give private or group lessons to teach a subject or skill that you are good at.
- Work additional hours (possibly off-times, such as evenings or weekends).
- Take on side work in addition to your regular occupation.

Here are some general suggestions for **reducing expenses:**

- Use cash exclusively.
- Look for cheaper service providers in all areas – from your phone company to your cleaning help to your dentist.
- Make a shopping list before you buy groceries, including quantities of each item.
- Don't go shopping when you're hungry, in a rush, or feeling down.
- Buy cheaper generic brands instead of brand names.
- Find creative, low-cost alternatives to expensive family outings.

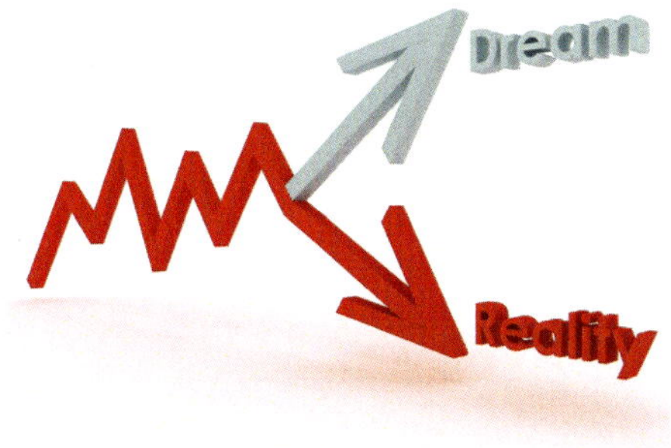

I want to turn my negative annual balance into a positive balance. How do I decide what budgetary changes to make?

Now that your income and expenses are neatly itemized in the monthly and annual budget forms, you should review each income item and decide whether it can be increased; look for ways to bring in income from new sources; and review each expense item and decide whether it can be reduced or removed. Don't be embarrassed to ask others for their advice when deciding what budgetary changes to make.

But be realistic when making these decisions. Try not to make drastic or sweeping budget cuts, since these typically cause severe stress in the home and are rarely sustainable long-term. Small, localized cuts are usually less painful and more easily implemented.

In general, increasing income is a better way to improve your annual balance than cutting expenses, since the potential for increasing income is theoretically unlimited, and increasing income may involve less stress. It is difficult to plan a budget based on possible increases in income, though, so be very careful when inflating your income projections for the future.

The process of making changes to your current budget often involves much trial and error, so do not be discouraged if your planned budget cuts or hoped-for increases in income do not materialize as you would have liked. If your first attempts at improving your annual balance don't work out the way you would like, keep on trying! You'll get there, with Hashem's help.

Monthly Budget

(Current/Projected)

A. Monthly Income

	Source: Salary/Wages (net)	Amount		Source: Interest/Dividends	Amount	Other Sources	Amount	Other Sources	Amount
Husband			Investment type			Rent			
						Child benefits			
						Unemployment benefits			
Wife						Social Security / Social Insurance			
						Pension/Retirement Fund			

Total Monthly Income

$

B. Monthly Expenses*

Expense Category	Amount	% of Total Expenditure
1: Housing		
2: Food & Household Items		
3: Bills & Utilities		
4: Education & Children		
5: Transportation		
6: Health & Personal Care		
7: Leisure		
8: Miscellaneous		

* See itemized list of expenses on next page.

Space for Calculations

Total Monthly Expenses

$

C. Monthly Balance

Total Monthly Income (end of section A)		Total Monthly Expenses (end of section B)		circle	Monthly Balance
$	−	$	=	+ / −	» $

Itemized List of Expenses for Section B of Monthly Budget

Item 1: Housing	
Rent	
Mortgage	
Property tax	
Building dues	
Cleaning help	
Outdoor maintenance	
Other	
Total:	

Item 2: Food & Household Items	
Meat & fish	
Fruits & vegetables	
Bread & baked goods	
Packaged foods	
Beverages	
Snack foods	
Restaurant & takeout	
Health food	
Household items	
Paper goods	
Cleaning supplies	
Other	
Total:	

Item 3: Bills & Utilities	
Social Security / Social Insurance	
Telephone	
Cell phone	
Electricity	
Gas / Heating oil	
Water	
Life insurance	
Appliance service contracts	
Bank charges	
Credit card charges	
Interest charges	
Other	
Total:	

Item 4: Education & Children	
School tuition / playgroup	
Daycare	
School transportation	
Babysitting	
Private lessons	
Tutoring	
Baby items	
Pocket money	
Support for single children	
Support for married children	
Other	
Total:	

Item 5: Transportation	
Auto lease	
Gasoline	
Tolls	
Buses	
Taxis	
Carpool	
Other	
Total:	

Item 6: Health & Personal Care	
Health insurance	
Medicines	
Vitamins	
Fitness	
Therapies	
Alternative medicine	
Contact lenses & solutions	
Toiletries & cosmetics	
Health & beauty treatments	
Haircuts	
Other	
Total:	

Item 7: Leisure	
Newspapers & magazines	
Gifts	
Flowers	
Stationery & crafts	
Lottery & raffle tickets	
Entertainment	
Other	
Total:	

Item 8: Miscellaneous	
Tzedakah	
Support for parents	
Savings plan	
Dry cleaning	
Pet expenses	
Other	
Total:	

Annual Budget

(Current/Projected)

D. Periodic Income

Periodic Income	Amount	Comments
Year-end bonus		
Tax refund		
Government benefits		
Charitable assistance		
Gifts		

Reduction of Income	Amount	Comments
Nissan		
Summer		
Tishrei		

Periodic Income $ – Reduction of Income $ = Total Periodic Income $

E. Periodic Expenses*

Expense Category	Amount	% of Total Expenditure
1: Housing		
2: Clothing		
3: Education & Children		
4: Transportation		
5: Health & Personal Care		
6: Holidays		
7: Leisure		
8: Miscellaneous		

Space for Calculations

* See itemized list of expenses on next page. Record only those expenses that are not included in your monthly budget.

Total Periodic Expenses $

F. Periodic Balance

Total Periodic Income (end of section D) $ – Total Periodic Expenses (end of section E) $ = circle + – Periodic Balance $

G. Annual Balance

Monthly Balance (end of section C on Monthly Budget) $ × 12 $

+ Periodic Balance (end of section F) $

= circle + – Annual Balance $

÷ 12 circle + – Adjusted Monthly Balance $

Itemized List of Expenses for Section E of Annual Budget

Item 1: Housing	
Homeowner's insurance	
Heating oil/gas	
Home repairs	
Appliance purchases	
Appliance repairs	
Furniture	
Lighting	
Kitchen supplies	
Pest control	
Other	
Total:	

Item 2: Clothing	
Clothing – parents	
Clothing – children	
Shoes – parents	
Shoes – children	
Jewelry & accessories	
Outerwear	
Head coverings	
Wig care	
Other	
Total:	

Item 3: Education & Children	
Enrichment for children	
Courses & classes	
School activities & other costs	
School supplies	
Summer camp	
Day camp	
Other	
Total:	

Item 4: Transportation	
Car insurance	
Car inspection & licensing	
Car repair & maintenance	
Emissions testing	
Parking & tickets	
Shipping	
Postage	
Other	
Total:	

Item 5: Health & Personal Care	
Medical expenses	
Medical equipment	
Dental & orthodontic	
Glasses	
Contact lenses	
Other	
Total:	

Item 6: Holidays	
Tishrei:	
Arbaat Haminim	
Succah	
Synagogue seats	
Holiday food	
Clothing & shoes	
Chol Hamoed outings	
Other	
Total - Tishrei:	
Purim:	
Mishloach Manot	
Matanot L'evyonim	
Costumes	
Gifts	
Other	
Total – Purim:	
Passover:	
Matzah	
Holiday food – general	
Wine	
Fruit & vegetables	
Meat & fish	
Cleaning help & supplies	
Dishes & utensils	
Clothing & shoes	
Chol Hamoed outings	
Afikoman presents	
Other	
Total – Passover:	
Shavuot	
Chanukah	
Tu b'Shevat	
Other	
Total - all holidays:	

Item 7: Leisure	
Vacations	
Summer residence	
Recreation	
Electronics	
Sports & hobbies	
Toys & games	
Music	
Gifts	
Photography	
parties and affairs	
Other	
Total:	

Item 8: Miscellaneous	
Tzedakah	
Shul dues	
Aliyot	
Seforim & books	
Computer equipment	
Personal article insurance	
Government documentation	
Other	
Total:	

The Next Frontier: Building a Cash Flow Plan

To keep your finances under control, it's not enough to build a budget. You also need to prepare a cash flow plan. A cash flow plan is simply a way of ensuring that you'll have the money you need, when you need it.

Why is this necessary? Because expenses – and in some cases, income – fluctuate from month to month. Even if your annual budget is balanced and you are earning enough money over the year to cover all of your expenses, you may still find yourself short on cash during peak-expense seasons such as Yamim Tovim or summer vacation.

A cash flow plan will help to ensure that when these peak-expense seasons arrive, you have enough money on hand to cover your bills. It will also help you to determine how much money you need to set aside during low-expense months to carry you through higher-expense months.

For people who do not earn regular monthly salaries, a cash flow plan is even more critical. A real estate agent might earn $10,000 in commissions one month, but nothing for the next two months. A freelancer who does not receive employee benefits might bring home a respectable income during months that have twenty-plus work days, but very little during months that include numerous sick or vacation days. A clothing store owner might post impressive revenues at the beginning of the winter and summer seasons, but have pitifully low mid-season sales. To make matters worse, peak-income seasons do not always coincide with peak-expense seasons; in fact, many self-employed people experience a significant drop in income during peak-expense seasons. (For instance, a musician may not have much work during the Three Weeks, but he still has to pay for his children's summer camp...)

Often, people whose income fluctuates exhibit a "feast/famine" lifestyle pattern, in which they live well during peak-income months, and experience severe financial strain during months when income slows to a trickle. This is extremely stressful, and quite avoidable. To ride out the peaks and troughs of irregular income, you need to develop a cash flow plan that will help you spread your income across the year.

Now that we've discussed budgeting, we will go on to an explanation of how to use your budget as a basis for a cash flow plan.

How do I build a cash flow plan?

When planning your budget, you made proactive decisions as to how you want to spend your money, within the boundaries created by your income. Now that you have a balanced budget, you also have to make sure that you will have enough money on hand to pay for the items included in your budget in a timely manner.

Don't rely on your wallet, or your bank account, to tell you what you can or can't afford. If you listen to your wallet instead of your budget, you're likely to spend money frivolously when your wallet is full and be overly tightfisted when your wallet is empty.

How do you make sure that your wallet is working in tandem with your budget, so that you have the right amount of money at the right time? That's the job of your cash flow plan.

The form entitled "Cash Flow Plan" is designed to help you calculate your projected cash flow and make any necessary adjustments.

In order to build a cash flow plan, you will need to calculate approximately how much money will be coming in (positive cash flow) and how much money will be going out (negative cash flow) during each of the next twelve months.

It is important to realize that **positive cash flow is not synonymous with income, and negative cash flow is not synonymous with expenses**. A person can have lots of income, and yet have negative cash flow – for instance, if his wages are delayed or if his money is tied up in investments and therefore inaccessible. Conversely, a person can have little or no income, and yet have positive cash flow – for instance, if he borrows money or liquidates his assets. (Keep in mind, however, that borrowed money quickly turns into negative cash flow when the time comes to repay it...)

Examples of positive cash flow items: +

- Income that is *paid* (not owed) to you
- Monetary gifts
- Revenue from the liquidation of assets
- Money that you borrow

Examples of negative cash flow items: –

- All purchases and payments
- Automated withdrawals from your bank account
- Money you put in savings or investments
- Debt repayments

Here is a step-by-step guide to building your cash flow plan:

Step 1:

Estimate the timing of annual income and expenses

When you built your budget plan, you differentiated between *monthly* income and expenses and *annual* (or *periodic*) income and expenses. Now, go through your itemized list of annual income and expenses and try to determine in which month each income or expense item belongs. The timing of certain annual budget items (such as holiday expenses, or summer camp) is easy to predict, while other items are difficult or impossible to predict; you do not know, for instance, when you might need to pay for a home repair. Annual budget items whose timing is predictable should be entered on the form under the month in which they are likely to happen.All other annual income and expenses should be added up separately and recorded as "remainder."

Step 2:

Estimate all other projected cash flow for each month

To estimate your projected cash flow for each month, you need to account for all projected positive and negative cash flow during that month. Your cash flow projections for any given month should include:

- Your regular monthly income and expenses
- The portion of your annual income and expenses that you anticipate during that month (which you calculated in step 1 above)
- Any other money that might be coming in or going out during that month (including a portion of your annual remainder, if applicable – see next paragraph).

The remainder you calculated in step one, representing the sum of all annual budget items whose timing is unpredictable, has to be assigned to the various months of the year. You can do this by dividing the total remainder by 12 and adding that figure (one-twelfth of the total remainder) to each month's cash flow figures. Alternatively, you can assign the remainder of your annual expenses to the first two or three months of the year and the remainder of your annual income to the last two or three months to ensure that you are prepared for unpredictable expenses whenever they happen. This money should be put aside in a place that is readily accessible, but not *too* accessible, to ensure that you are not tempted to use it for other purposes.

Obviously, your cash flow estimates will be far from perfect. Unpredictable annual expenses might all happen in the beginning of the year; they might all happen at the end of the year; or they might happen at various times throughout the year. They certainly won't cooperate with your cash flow plan and divide themselves evenly over the twelve months of the year. **Because you have no way of knowing when these expenses will**

happen, the best you can do is give a reasonable estimate. It is therefore important that you monitor your actual cash flow throughout the year and make any necessary midcourse corrections.

Step 3:

Calculate your projected monthly cash flow balance

Once you have those estimates, the next step is to calculate your projected cash flow balance for each of the next twelve months, using the following formula:

> **Total positive cash flow**
> **– Total negative cash flow**
> **= Cash flow balance**

A positive balance in a particular month means that you will have a surplus during that month; a negative balance means that you will have a deficit during that month.

You now have a cash flow projection for the next twelve months.

Step 4:

Make adjustments for negative cash flow periods

Based on your cash flow projection, you can go on to make adjustments to compensate for the period(s) in which you anticipate a negative cash flow.

Adjusting for negative cash flow means finding a source from which to finance the deficit you are anticipating during a given period. If the period in which you anticipate negative cash flow comes after a period of positive cash flow, the best thing to do is to put aside money during the positive cash flow period to tide you over the negative cash flow period. But if the negative cash flow period comes first, or if you are unable to put aside enough money during the positive cash flow period to tide you through the negative cash flow period, then you will need to find an alternate financing source. This source can be either internal (liquidating your own savings, investments, or assets) or external (taking interim loans or credit). In most cases, tapping into your own resources is preferable to borrowing from an external source.

Does it matter whether I start my cash flow plan in a positive cash flow month or a negative cash flow month?

A cash flow plan is meant to empower you to ride out the budgetary fluctuations that inevitably occur throughout the year. Therefore, it is worthwhile to begin a cash flow plan in a position of strength, with cash in hand to tide you through the negative cash flow period ahead, rather than begin the plan with a deficit and constantly have to look back and cover past expenses.

If it is not possible to jumpstart the cash flow plan with cash in hand, however, then it is important to plan *how much* money you will need to cover your negative cash flow, *where* you will take it from, and *how* and *when* you will pay it back. Planning cash flow financing carefully will enable you to borrow or withdraw only the amount you actually need, and ensure that you have a way to repay the loan or replenish your resources.

Cash Flow Plan

A. Projected Annual/Periodic Expenses by Month

In section E of the Annual Budget, you entered totals for each of the eight periodic expense categories listed. Now, calculate what portion of those periodic expense categories can be assigned to specific months and record the amounts below. The portion of the periodic expense categories that is unpredictable should be recorded under "Remainder."

For instance: Most purchases in the clothing category typically take place at the beginning of the winter and summer seasons, so you might assign 40% of your clothing budget to the month of September and 40% to the month of April, and then record the remaining 20% under "Remainder," since you don't know in which month you will incur the remaining clothing expenses.

Month	Projected Expense: Category 1 - Housing	Projected Expense: Category 2 - Clothing	Projected Expense: Category 3 - Education & Children	Projected Expense: Category 4 - Transportation	Projected Expense: Category 5 - Health & Personal Care	Projected Expense: Category 6 - Holidays	Projected Expense: Category 7 - Leisure	Projected Expense: Category 8 - Miscellaneous	Total Projected Expenses: All categories
Month 1									
Month 2									
Month 3									
Month 4									
Month 5									
Month 6									
Month 7									
Month 8									
Month 9									
Month 10									
Month 11									
Month 12									
Total									
Grand Total*									
Remainder (Grand total - Total)									

* Take these figures from section E of Annual Budget.

This is the sum of the projected expense amounts listed above for the 12 months of the year.

Flip back to Section E of the Annual Budget, and transfer to this row the figures listed in the eight categories of the Amount column.

This figure shows the portion of each periodic expense category that is unpredictable. You can't know exactly when these expenses will crop up.

B. Cash Position by Month

In this table, enter monthly estimates for each of the positive and negative cash flow categories and calculate the monthly balance. If the monthly balance is negative, indicate how you plan to cover the deficit by recording the proposed adjustment source and amount.

	Positive cash flow				Negative cash flow								
Month	Projected Monthly Income	Projected Annual/ Periodic Income	Remainder	Other	Projected Monthly Expenses	Projected Annual/ Periodic Expenses (from Table A above)	Savings Plan	Debt Repay-ment	Remainder	Other	Monthly Balance	Adjustment Source	Adjustment Amount
Month 1													
Month 2													
Month 3													
Month 4													
Month 5													
Month 6													
Month 7													
Month 8													
Month 9													
Month 10													
Month 11													
Month 12													

The Final Challenge: Divide & Conquer

The following is an article that appeared in Mesila's Hamodia column.

A Tale of Two Incomes — and a Deficit

Question:

Our financial situation was always such that we never were able to make ends meet. For the first few years after we got married, my husband learned in was still in school. We lived very frugally then, but we nevertheless got into debt. When my husband began working part-time, we moved to a different community, where our expenses increased, and so did our debt. We were running to gemachim constantly. Eventually, my husband got a full-time job in a brokerage firm with an income that started at about $25,000 a year (this goes back some twenty years). At that time, the income was inadequate to cover our expenses, and we got ourselves into serious credit card debt.

Over the years, our income has increased. I became a dental hygienist several years ago so I bring home about $3,000 a month, which does help a lot. Our total monthly take home income is presently $10,160, plus my husband's year-end bonus of $10,000.

We still owe a lot of back taxes, and we have a monthly arrangement to pay these taxes. But we often end up buying food with post-dated checks, and we still occasionally get shut off notices from the utility companies. Our financial situation has caused my husband major stress and has really affected the atmosphere in our home.

I'm concerned that we may be really mismanaging our money, since considering our income, we should be managing comfortably. When I list the expenses, though, it looks as though we need several thousand dollars a month more.

Our monthly expenses (not including food, groceries, clothing, holiday costs, gifts, etc.) are $9,346, itemized below:

Mortgage:	*$2,250*
Property taxes:	*$700*
Gas and electric:	*$600*
Water:	*$80*
Cleaners:	*$120*
Tuition for two children:	*$1,050*
School transportation:	*$230*
Allowance for son learning in Israel:	*$400*
Cleaning help:	*$320*
Pay back on down payment for house:	*$300*
Gemach payments:	*$925*
Income tax (owed from past):	*$350*
Car payments:	*$516*
Car insurance:	*$300*
Gasoline:	*$350*
Homeowners' insurance:	*$125*
Credit card debt (old):	*$250*
Credit card payments:	*$120 (just interest)*
Medicine:	*$100*
Telephone:	*$100*
Cell phones (3):	*$160*

Any help or advice that you can offer would be greatly appreciated.

Mesila's response:

We welcome your inquiry, and we will be happy to assist you to the best of our ability. The situation you describe is all too common, particularly in the U.S.: two parents working hard to earn a respectable combined income, yet struggling to meet their financial obligations.

Mesila's counseling program involves three stages, the first and most basic of which is helping a family become aware of its exact financial situation. You have done an excellent job coming up with a detailed budget breakdown, and we congratulate you on taking this first step towards financial stability. Because you have provided us with a breakdown of your budget, we can hopefully zero in on the source of the problem and offer some suggestions for solving it.

What seems to be preventing you from achieving financial stability is the fact that about 20% of your income is going towards repayment of old debts – not including your mortgage – so you continually have to borrow money to cover your ongoing living expenses.

The way Mesila recommends that you break this vicious cycle is by separating debt from living expenses, using what we call the "divide and conquer approach." Debts and living expenses have to be viewed as two distinct financial obligations and managed as two separate accounts. Your income is meant to cover your living expenses, and your debts have to be paid for from a separate fund.

In the budget breakdown you sent us, debts are lumped together with living expenses and are not itemized. (For instance, when you say "Gemach payments," how many *gemachim* are you paying and how much do you owe to each of them?) The first thing you need to do, therefore, is create a separate, itemized list of debts.

The second thing you need to do is ensure that your annual income is covering your annual living expenses. You have done a good job of itemizing a portion of your monthly expenses above, but it is crucial that you add food, groceries, clothing, holiday expenses, gifts, and whatever is included in "etc." to your list so that you can determine how much you are really spending. You also need to account for annual and occasional expenses (such as summer camp, or car and home repairs), so that your figures reflect the true annual picture of your finances, rather than a narrow monthly slice of the yearly expense pie.

Once you have accurate figures of your annual income and expenses, you will be able to calculate your annual balance by subtracting expenses from income. If the balance is positive, then you have an annual budget surplus, and you can move on to build a long-term debt repayment plan. If your balance is zero, slightly more than zero, or negative, then you will have to work on increasing your income and/or decreasing your expenditures so that you can carve out a budget surplus, which will become your debt repayment fund.

Whether your annual balance is positive, negative, or zero, you should never use borrowed money to pay for living expenses. Borrowed money includes post-dated checks, installment plans, buying on credit at local stores, and even credit cards, if you are carrying over a balance from month to month. It is critical that your living expenses be covered by your income, to ensure that your debts do not continue to mount. A family that runs an ongoing monthly deficit is headed for financial disaster, so if you find that your income is not covering your living expenses, then you will have to implement emergency measures – which may include working overtime, implementing spending cuts, or even taking *tzedakah* – to close the gap.

We are hopeful, however, that your living expenses *can* be covered by your income, considering that you are earning a very respectable net income of $10,160 a month. Assuming that this is the case, then once you have calculated your annual budget surplus, you can work on creating a fund for debt repayment. This is done by allocating money for all of your living expenses, and then building a long-term debt repayment plan based on your annual budget surplus, which is the amount you can afford to put towards debt repayment every year.

To illustrate, let's say your annual budget surplus is $10,000. If that is the case, you may decide to repay $833 ($10,000 divided by 12) every month. Or, you may decide that you prefer to repay $1,000 ten times a year, so that you do not have to make debt repayments around the times of Pesach and Succos, when your expenses are higher and your income might be reduced. Either way, your debt will be reduced by $10,000 a year. If you find that you can afford to channel more money into your debt repayment fund as time goes on, that is wonderful, but you have to be very careful that paying extra does not result in financial hardship that will lead you to take on more debts or abandon your debt repayment plan because it is too constricting.

In order to create your debt repayment plan, you will probably have to renegotiate the repayment terms of some of the old debts so that your monthly payments can be tailored to an amount that reflects your annual budget surplus. Another option is to consolidate your debt by taking out one large loan to pay off all of the old debts. If you decide to take out a new loan to consolidate your debt, make sure that (a) the monthly payments do not exceed the amount that can afford to repay and (b) the new loan is exactly equal to the amount you owe. (If it is more than you currently owe, your debt will increase; if it is less than you currently owe, you will still be saddled with the burden of repaying multiple debts.)

The advantage of paying back your debts in this manner is that you are able to eliminate your debts as quickly as you can afford to without having to take on any new debts in the interim and without severely compromising your standard of living.

Please realize, however, that the plan that we have just outlined is purely theoretical. To create a realistic, workable plan, you need to invest time and effort to build the plan. As time goes on, you will also need to continually reevaluate your financial situation and your debt load and fine-tune the plan based on your changing financial realities.

Because building – and following – such a plan is challenging, we strongly recommend that you either find someone whom you trust to act as your financial counselor, or apply for Mesila's assistance.

The road to financial stability is often long and arduous, but you seem to be organized, disciplined and motivated enough to succeed in the journey. Feel free to contact us with any further questions.

As we saw in the above article, *A Tale of Two Incomes – and a Deficit*, a common budgeting pitfall is allowing different elements of your finances to get mixed up. In order to really know what's going on and manage your money correctly, you need to differentiate between the following:

Income: Money **coming in** that belongs to you

Assets: Money or property that you currently own

Liabilities: Money that you owe or property that causes you loss

Expenses: Money that you spend as part of your living costs

Maintaining Order – The Divide-and-Conquer Approach

Distinguishing between the many aspects of your finances – which Mesila calls the "divide-and-conquer approach" – is important for two reasons: it helps you to gain an awareness of exactly what is happening with your money, and it puts you in control of your finances by enabling you to make informed decisions.

To implement the divide-and-conquer approach, you should differentiate assets from ongoing income, and debt from ongoing expenses. Loans cannot be considered income, nor can their repayment be considered a living expense. Managing debts and living expenses as two separate accounts will make it possible to get a clear picture of what is going on in each account, and will allow you to achieve control over both accounts in an efficient, orderly manner.

The divide-and-conquer approach extends to other aspects of your finances as well. One-time sources of income have to be differentiated from ongoing or occasional income, and one-time expenses have to be differentiated from your ongoing budget. This ensures that your estimated monthly or annual income is not artificially inflated by a one-time windfall, and that your estimated monthly or annual expenses are not artificially inflated by a one-time outlay.

Similarly, if you have a business, it has to be treated as a separate account. When business and family finances become mixed together, it becomes impossible to reach awareness of what is happening in either one. Separating business finances from family finances makes it possible to reach awareness of what is happening in both, which in turn allows each of them to be managed effectively.

In summary, Mesila uses the divide-and-conquer approach to differentiate between:

- Monthly, annual, occasional and one-time sources of income
- Income and assets
- Living expenses and debt
- Monthly, annual, occasional and one-time expenses
- Business and family finances

Once you have differentiated between these elements of your finances, you will be able to isolate problematic areas from non-problematic areas. Seeing that you are succeeding in at least some areas of your financial management will give you the confidence and motivation to extend your success to other, more problematic areas.

After identifying the areas of your finances that are in need of improvement, you will be in a position to develop distinct strategies to deal with each of those areas.

Financial problems often seem overwhelming, with no solutions in sight. In Mesila's experience, however, even the most complex problems can become manageable if they are broken down into individual, distinct problems and tackled piece by piece.

Divide & Conquer Exercise

The purpose of the following exercise is:

1. To differentiate between the various elements of a family's finances
2. To learn that income has to be designated first for ongoing living expenses to prevent debt from accumulating. (If you use your income to repay debt, you may have to borrow to pay living expenses.)
3. To learn that assets are intended for future or one-time expenses such as buying a home, making weddings, retirement, etc.

Instructions: Categorize each of the items at the bottom of this page into the four categories of the table below.

Income	Assets	Expenses	Liabilities

Bank charges
Bank overdraft
Birthday money
Bonds
Cash
Certificates of deposits (CDs)
Checking accounts
Commissions
Credit card balance
Credit card fees
Debts
Fellowship grant/stipend
Gifts to others
Grocery account
Home
Income tax
Insurance deductible
IRA/401 (k)/RRSP – Canada
Loans owed to you
Mortgage
Mutual funds
Parental support/allowance
Paycheck
Personal valuables (jewelry, etc.)
Post-dated checks
Properties
Property tax
Rent
Retirement funds
Savings accounts
Stocks/shares
Stock dividends
Student loans
Summer residence
Tax refund
Tuition
Tzedakah
Vacations

I have a budget, a cash flow plan, and I've gotten things organized. Now what?

Now that you have created a workable budget and cash flow plan, you need to continue tracking your cash flow for several months until you are sure that your projections are in line with the reality.

About halfway through each month, you should tally all positive and negative cash flow since the beginning of that month. Compare these numbers to your cash flow projections for the month, and see whether you are on target to stay within your budget. If you notice that you are deviating from your budget, now is the time to make a midcourse correction, either by finding a way to increase your income for the month or by spending less than you had planned for the remainder of the month.

If you find yourself consistently deviating from your budget or cash flow plan – in either direction – that is an indication that your budget needs to be reworked. If you are frequently spending more than your budget allows, you may have to recalculate your expenses and adjust your budget to more accurately reflect your true expenses. If you are frequently spending less than your budget allows, you might want to consider upping the amount you designate for savings.

Once you have successfully followed your budget for several months, and you have seen that your income and expense projections are accurate, you may choose to stop tracking your financial transactions on a daily, item-by-item basis. Nevertheless, you should still keep a basic record of how much money is coming in and how much is going out each month, to ensure that you are remaining within your budget and cash flow plan. In addition, when you are anticipating a costly occasion (such as a wedding, or moving to a new home) or a high-expense season (such as Pesach or summer vacation), you should track each expense associated with that particular occasion or season so that you can determine exactly how much you spent. This will help you plan for future occasions, and will also allow you to separate ongoing expenses from one-time expenses so that you can determine whether you have stayed within your regular budget for ongoing expenses.

After your budget is in place and working well, you and your spouse should schedule regular meetings – monthly, or at least quarterly – to assess whether you have stayed within your budget and, if necessary, adjust your budget to reflect your family's changing circumstances.

Long-term Budgeting

Until now, we have been talking about building a short-term budget, which is basically a one-year financial plan that reflects your current income and expenses and also includes provisions for savings (and debt repayment, if necessary).

Ideally, however, your budget should be composed of two parts: a short-term budget and a long-term budget. A long-term budget is less detailed than a short-term budget, simply because it is not possible to make accurate budgetary predictions for the distant future.

To build a long-term budget, you need to look ahead and consider what major expenses you anticipate during the next few years: Do you have a child who is going to need orthodontic work? Are you planning to renovate your house? Are you hoping to make a wedding?

Your long-term budget should include savings for any large, foreseeable expenses during the next few years, and it should include savings for unforeseeable expenses as well. This way, when you encounter an unexpected financial pitfall – e.g., your car breaks down, or you require a medical procedure that your insurance does not cover – you will be prepared. We have to expect the unexpected, because unexpected expenses happen to everyone. The only things that are unexpected about unexpected expenses is *what* they will be and *when* they will happen – not *whether* they will happen.

Your long-term budget should also include provisions for anticipated increases or decreases in income .And if you are in debt ,your long-term budget must include a realistic strategy for repaying *all* of your debts.

How do I know if my budget is **workable?**

In order for a budget to work, it has to be realistic and somewhat flexible. If unbudgeted-for expenses continually arise, or if routine expenses consistently exceed their budgeted allotment, those are indications that the budget is too restrictive and needs to be reworked.

A good budget is one that does all of the following:

- Generously covers all essentials
- Leaves some room for non-essentials
- Makes provisions for unanticipated expenses
- Incorporates both short- and long-term savings

This type of budget creates financial structure, takes the focus in the home off money issues and contributes to an environment in which healthy family relationships can flourish.

Living with a budget requires discipline, but it should not make you feel deprived. If you have indeed created a realistic budget, you should be able to acquire all of the things you *need*, and some – but probably not all – of the things you *want*. Nobody has everything they want, but if you build your budget correctly, you'll be able to have the things that are most important to you, and you should not feel that you are missing much by forgoing the things that you have left out of your budget.

Overview:
Steps of Budgeting

The main steps involved in building a budget and cash flow plan are:

1. Determine your total income.
2. Track your expenses for several months.
3. Group expenses into major categories.
4. Calculate your annual budget balance.
5. Decide what budgetary changes you wish to make.
6. Build your budget plan, ensuring that you have a budgetary surplus.
7. Estimate positive and negative cash flow for each of the next 12 months.
8. Calculate your cash flow balance for each of the next 12 months.
9. Make adjustments for negative cash flow periods.
10. Give your budget a test run, tweaking it as necessary.
11. Continually review your budget and adjust it to reflect new realities.
12. Build a long-term budget.

family*feature*

Downsize to upgr

The Art of Living with Less

A table, some chairs, a folding cot — our succahs pass the minimalist test with flying colors. And for good reason: one of the themes of the Yom Tov is redefining our relationship with the physical. And the lessons we learn need not vanish once we take down our succahs; downsizing can enrich our lives both physically and emotionally

Reprinted with Permission from Mishpacha Jewish Family Weekly

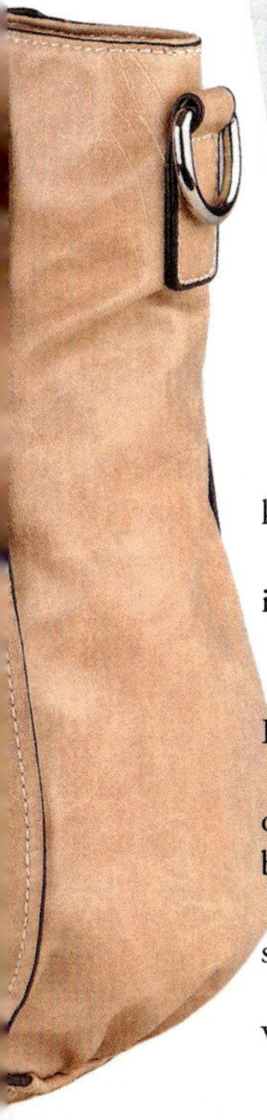

MICHAL EISIKOWITZ

On January 12, 2005, Raizy Weiss's* bedroom fixture exploded. Though firefighters fought hard to contain the flames, she watched from the street corner as an electric fire ravaged the entire second floor of her home.

Traumatized — yet deeply grateful the loss was only material — Raizy numbly set out to build a wardrobe and furniture set from scratch. Once the dust settled and the shock subsided, she made an astonishing discovery: apart from two *sheitels* and a cherished set of her children's baby pictures, she wasn't missing much.

"Virtually nothing destroyed was really valuable to me," she relates. "Most of what was burned, I never used."

Surprising? Not for someone like ardent minimalist Everett Bogue.

"It's like 'What do I actually use in my daily life?' " Everett exclaims while revealing a totally empty cabinet in his stark-would-be-an-understatement kitchen.

A devotee of the "100 Thing Challenge," a group whose members aim to own no more than one hundred items, Everett owns a total of fifty-seven items, including a bed, a couch, and a laptop computer. His raison d'etre is "less is more" — and he's awfully proud of it.

"Two pots, two pans, a pair of shoes," says a smiling Everett as he shows off five of his paltry panoply of possessions.

Readers may be wagging their heads, wondering why yet another nutty fellow is being gloriously wheeled into the spotlight. But statistics show Everett may not be as loopy as you think.

According to the National Association of Professional Organizers, the average person uses only 20 percent of what he owns, and wears 20 percent of his clothing 80 percent of the time. If that's the case, we stuff-lovers might be the fools around here, insisting on cluttering our homes — and our brainspace.

"I began to feel lighter and freer," attests Jenn DiPiazza, a former packrat who embarked on an all-out downsizing campaign after an eye-opening stay in a spartan Navajo reservation. "I was no longer weighed down by all this stuff."

Everett and Jenn are not alone in their quest for simplicity. The "buy no more" mindset is gaining momentum, asserts professional organizer Peter Walsh, due in large part to the recession. While not everybody is downsizing voluntarily, almost everyone is trying to make do with less.

"We're moving to a deeper level of contentment and happiness that's not tied to the accumulation of stuff," says Mr. Walsh.

* *Name has been changed*

Personal downsizing is "in." That's good news for the Jews, since Chazal have long enumerated the virtues of simple living. So while you may not be ready to slash your possessions to the double-digit level, downscaling offers unique benefits that adherents claim have greatly enhanced their quality of life — both physical and spiritual.

WHY DOWNSIZE?

On hearing of the stuff-slimming trend, the first question for many individuals is "why bother?" Downsizing takes time and effort — and emotionally, it's not always a breeze.

But fans of the practice insist that the liberating feeling engendered is worth the price.

"It's a catalyst for freedom," writes "Simply Stephen," a personal downsizing guru. "One can enjoy the things they have more. Cupboards have space. Life has less clutter. It takes less time to maintain everything."

Directing energies towards downsizing can also change personal spending habits: stuff doesn't make you happy anymore.

"An abundant life can be spent *doing* things instead of *acquiring* things," says Stephen.

Mrs. Zlata Press, principal of Brooklyn's Prospect Park Bnos Leah High School, takes this a step further with a thought from the Netziv (*HaEmek Davar, Devarim* 4:1): "Materialism stresses the importance of 'things' and devalues the importance of spirit," she paraphrases. "Downsizing, on the other hand, allows one to focus on life's real pleasures."

Still others find that downsizing offers enormous practical benefits: more space, plus the peace of mind knowing the location of each of your possessions.

"It's the *nachas* of a clean, clutter-free desk," muses Edna Deblinger,* a mother and grandmother. Edna — owner of a spacious but furniture-filled home — can't claim to have downsized on the scale she'd like, but she's trying. "Over the years, I've learned that not having to struggle to find what you need each morning is a huge thing."

The case for downsizing becomes even more compelling when you face the facts that most of what we have, we don't use.

Shlomo* came to this realization by accident. Before a move overseas, he got rid of 10 percent of his stuff and stored the rest. When he returned, he realized that most of it wasn't missed.

"I hadn't needed it; it served no purpose," remembers Shlomo, who since became a hard-core downsizer.

Indeed, some individuals discover that the magic of minimalism lies in the economical distribution of resources.

"Our joy comes from the fact that we're not wasting," writes one aficionado. "We could buy the best laundry detergent and it wouldn't break us. We could eat gourmet meals every night and our budget could handle it. We could just buy our kids new stuffed animals instead of making them. But we take a lot of pleasure out of frugal choices and frugal projects in our life."

A Lakewood mother of three, Rena Kellner* echoes these sentiments. She and her husband grew up in financially comfortable homes where they never felt the pinch. As their family grew, however, and resources dwindled, reality hit hard.

"At first, the downsizing and lowering of our *hasagos* was extremely difficult," she admits candidly. "But after a while, we got used to the new routines and even started liking some."

Which brings us to the most common, irrefutable rationale for downsizing: not enough cash. Instead of ending the month in the red, many money-strapped families choose to take charge of their financial destiny by downgrading — in a variety of ways. The results? Hundreds more dollars left in their pockets — or the serenity of soul that comes with staying clear of debt.

WHERE DO YOU START?

Okay, you're convinced. An inspiration to part with possessions wells within, but how to go about it?

It's a big one, but if you have the courage, you can join the millions of people who've chosen to downsize their homes. Once almost exclusively associated with empty-nesters and retirees looking for smaller spaces after the kids have moved out, this move is gaining popularity with a growing number of middle-aged, money-smart homeowners.

> According to the National Association of Professional Organizers, the average person uses only 20 percent of what he owns, and wears 20 percent of his clothing 80 percent of the time

"It just made sense for us at this point in our lives," says Canada-based Sari Coffman,* who moved with her husband of 35 years and youngest daughter from a spacious home to a rental duplex. "Owning the house was silly; even when all my marrieds came for Yom Tov the house was too small, and it was too big for us the rest of the year."

The Coffmans have seen firsthand the manifold cost-cutting benefits of home downsizing. For one, they save thousands of dollars each year in mortgage payments — generally the single largest expense consumers face — plus, they're freed from exorbitant property taxes — the next greatest homeowner's outlay.

A smaller place also means fewer dollars spent on utilities.

"Why am I paying to heat and cool an entire basement I never use?" wondered Brooklyn homeowner Risa Thaler* before opting to downsize.

What's more, home downsizing can cut household maintenance in half. Living in a condo, for example, means not having to mow your lawn each week. Fewer bedrooms to paint, for another, means painting job prices drop significantly.

Malka Forster* of Jerusalem remembers a humorous exchange she had with a neighbor shortly after her marriage. On hearing that Malka's apartment had four bedrooms, the *sabra* mother of seven exclaimed, "Why would you want that? It's *so* much to clean!"

"I struggled to keep a straight face," recalls Malka. "I thought, *Is this woman for real? Do I want to move into the likes of her tiny, two-bedroom*

"An abundant life can be spent *doing* things instead of *acquiring* things"

DOWNSIZING: THE PATH TO SPIRITUAL GREATNESS?
Questions and Answers with Rebbetzin Tziporah Heller

If a *frum* Jew was asked, "Does the Torah view downsizing favorably?" he'd probably answer affirmatively. Would you say this is a valid assumption?

It could be, but not necessarily. The Torah views the material world as a means to end; if a person has much – all acquired *b'heter*, all used *l'sheim Shamayim* – there's nothing wrong with that. *Not having* is not a goal. *Having* is not a goal. Using what you have in a way that's appropriate and suits your *avodas Hashem* is the goal.

There have always been people who chose minimal involvement with physical pleasure. A Yerushalmi tzaddik, for example, once tasted an apricot for the first time. He felt such exhilaration that he resolved never to eat an apricot again; the emotional attachment engendered from its taste distracted him from life's real goal.

And it's not just the rich who face the challenge of material attachment: often people with very little are at least as emotionally involved as wealthier individuals, if not more. For example, a minority teenager once killed another teen for his Nike sneakers. Neither teenager had lots of stuff, but clearly, they were deeply attached to "stuff."

Chazal say, "Increase your possessions, and increase your worry." Doesn't that statement clearly support downsizing?

This statement describes a practical reality; it's a nugget of wise advice, not necessarily or exclusively, a directive. The fact is that possessions exact time and space from their owners. The Rambam says that before a person buys something, he should calculate how much it will cost him – not only in money, but in mental energy and maintenance.

Who is a good candidate for downsizing?

Anyone who feels they've become emotionally involved with their things. And taking pride in *not* having – a growing trend in some circles – can also be a form of emotional involvement. Ideally, people should be too busy doing meaningful things with their lives to have time to dwell on assets – whether it's buying more of them or thinking about how few they have.

The *Yated* newspaper once ran a raffle in which every subscriber had a chance to win a variety of prizes. The sweepstakes was entirely computerized, a fact that yielded laughable results: The winner of a set of turquoise towels, as published in the paper, was a "Y.S. Elyashiv" from Yerushalayim. Now, try to envision Rav Elyashiv's *shlita* reaction upon hearing this news. Certainly he didn't say, "That's wonderful! Turquoise towels!" But the *posek hador's* likely indifferent response was not because turquoise towels aren't beautiful or wouldn't enhance his home; it's because he's occupied day and night with things far more eternal than turquoise towels.

An internationally renowned lecturer and author, Rebbetzin Heller's newest project is "Duties of the Heart," an online daily learning program of Chovos HaLevavos.

apartment because it means less sponja?"

Life, however, taught Malka some surprising things.

"As my family grew, and frequent, exhausting cleaning runs became a requisite part of my daily routine, I was finally able to hear her point," she concedes. "I'm not ready to downsize — my place is not that big, after all — but still, I've discovered the kernel of truth in her words."

So how *do* you know if your house is too big for you? One downsizer offers an ingenious gauge: "When two of your bathrooms are regularly dusted rather than cleaned because of non-use!"

For many homeowners, though, the thought of abandoning a house full of wonderful memories and uprooting to an entirely new locale is terrifying. How do downsizers overcome this hurdle?

"I took the most sentimental items with me," says Risa Thaler, whose home of 30 years was actually razed after she sold it, to make room for an all-new mansion. "But more importantly, I moved only a few blocks away. I live in the same community, daven in the same shul, and socialize with the same acquaintances. Now that I've moved, these long-time anchors in my life are what evoke the memories I treasure."

A widow for over a decade now, Risa points out another significant factor: she *chose* to downsize, wanting the security of living near others in an apartment building.

"Because the move was *my* initiative, the transition was easier. I knew this was best for me."

For Sari Coffman, moving into her three-bedroom rental was practically painless because she never developed an attachment to a particular home.

"Over my 35 years of marriage, I moved about ten times," she explains. "And by nature, I'm not an accumulator. When we relocated to Canada from Eretz Yisrael, I left almost everything there. It's not like I own a cherished 25-year-old crib that cradled all six of my children."

But even if she *had* lived in one home for many years, Sari believes she would've downsized anyway, if that's what made sense for her family. The insight Rav Pam *ztz"l* once gave her on a person's ideal relationship to his earthly abode still rings in her ears.

"We once hosted a dinner in our home that Rav Pam attended," recounts Sari. "At that point, we'd finally settled in Canada after fifteen years of marriage — and then my husband felt we should pick up and go to Eretz Yisrael. I was devastated; I'd been so thrilled to have established ourselves in a community.

"I turned to Rav Pam for an *eitzah*. 'This is so hard for me! What should we do?' I cried. Rav Pam listened to the reasoning on both sides and then looked me in the eye. 'Mrs. Coffman,' he said, 'a woman has to be happy with her husband and her children. If you have that, you can move anywhere.' "

JETTISON YOUR JUNK

Some readers will smile in satisfaction (or self-pity!) as they read this article. "Not for me," they think wryly. "I'm downsized to the last penny!" But whatever your financial state, there's the universally applicable, most basic form of downsizing: decluttering.

"Mess brings stress," asserts Yvonne Trostli, a psychotherapist who specializes in chronic disorganization. "You can't see the things that bring you delight because you have too many things to look at."

"We keep things because they're valuable," agrees aspiring downsizer Edna Deblinger, "but if you have to build a new closet or storage room for them, they lose their value."

How to decide what's tossed and what's treasured? According to Barry Izsak, president of the National Association of Professional Organizers and a certified senior move manager in Austin, Texas, anything worth keeping must meet one of the following three criteria: (a) it must be useful and used often; (b) it must be sentimental and extremely rare and special (if you have several such items from one person, you may want to let some go); or (c) it must add to the beauty of your home.

Transplanted New Yorker Shoshana Balaban says she's learned the art of decluttering from her Israeli neighbors, who are pros at living in smaller spaces.

"Before bringing an item into the house, my friends look at it with beady, critical eyes: 'Do we really need it? Where will it go?' For every item they take inside, two items are shipped out."

SIMPLIFYING: IT'S NOT ALWAYS SIMPLE

Despite its numerous benefits, however, no one claims that downsizing is painless. Particularly in today's consumerist climate, where we've been indoctrinated practically since birth to believe that we "need" an untold number of items to attain happiness, it's not easy to go against the tide.

Even psychotherapist Yvonne Trostli admits to a personal struggle. "One part of me that would love to live ...with sparse aesthetics is constantly squabbling with the part that loves the feeling of plenty that comes with a stocked refrigerator and ... a room surrounded by books and sacred objects all in full view."

It's normal to feel this paradox, says Ms. Trostli. But the more you practice letting go, the more familiar — and desirable — the terrain becomes.

"We haven't downsized, we've upsized," affirms Shoshana Balaban, who gave up a well-paying position and American-style home to live in Eretz Yisrael. "Letting go of the extra bandwidth required to maintain our possessions and lifestyle has enormously improved our quality of life."

Shoshana offers as an example the property the Balabans owned in the States. "I had dreams of a magnificent garden, but the land lay bare. I was working full-time and my husband learning; we didn't have the time or resources to tend to it."

Shoshana's current home, by contrast, is bordered by a modest balcony overlooking the verdant Judean Hills.

"It's got a few beautiful plants that we can realistically care for, and I'm thrilled," says Shoshana. "This garden is a fraction of the size, but it's so much more satisfying."

New York Times columnist David Brooks seems to agree, offering a slightly different take on the issue. During his family vacation to the Serengeti, he describes how the more luxurious lodging camps — with showers and pools — felt distinctly colder, while the simpler camps — some without electricity and running water — were warm and cozy.

"It occurred to me that when we moved from a simple camp to a more luxurious camp, we crossed an invisible Heimish Line," he writes.

This phenomenon applies to all aspects of life. Often, contends Mr. Brooks, spending more doesn't mean enjoying more.

"When we're shopping for a vacation we're primarily thinking about *Where* ... But when you come back from vacation, you primarily treasure the memories of *Who* — the people you met from faraway places, and the lives you came in contact with."

Yet another truth corroborating what's consistently emerged from years of happiness research: Better to buy *experiences* than *things*. In other words, memories of a well-planned but not-necessarily-costly Chol HaMoed family trip will be treasured long after the glamour of a new, stylish Yom Tov outfit fades away.

So as we step through the doorways of our succahs this year, leaving behind the creature comforts of our spacious, elegant homes, let's embrace the clarity of soul that comes with living a far more unadorned existence.

Shoshana sums it up as the gift of simplicity. "I have less stuff," she says, "but my life is richer." ■

The following material has been excerpted, with permission, from a series in ***Binah magazine*** *by* ***Shoshana Bernstein*** *entitled:*

A Balancing Act

Real families: Real facts, figures, fears and faith.

Stage 1: Newlyweds

For obvious reasons, names have been changed.

Debra and Raphael Weiss

Profile

Age: Late twenties

Years married: 2

Children: 1

Occupation:

Wife: Cosmetician

Husband: Start-up company

Financial arrangement

"Our parents generously help with rent and utilities, much to our chagrin. (We wish they didn't have to at all.)"

Monthly salary

Wife: $3000

"My husband has begun to set up a start-up company which will hopefully bring in more."

Monthly expenses

Rent:	$900
Utilities:	$300
Total covered by parents:	$1,200
Health Insurance: (plus co-pays)	$1000
Groceries: (staying home for Shabbat can be more)	$700
Taxes:	$600
Car Insurance:	$135
Gas:	$120
Phone/Internet:	$100
Total: $2,655	

Miscellaneous

We've been paying $350 a month to pay off the deductibles from our baby's birth. We made our final payment this month! Hooray!

Plus, every so often we go clothes shopping, buy "treats" and flowers for Shabbat, and gifts. Car repairs costs money and we are working on paying off our debt.

Debt

Credit card: $3500 (approximately)

We're actively working on it – it was accrued through unexpected emergency circumstances at the start of our marriage.

Savings

$20,000-30,000 – Wedding gifts, some money from before marriage

$3,000 – Gift money for the child in her own account

We try to put aside between $50 and $100 each month, no matter what.

Additional pertinent information

Summer work will hopefully pay off another chunk of debt… we both freelance too, trying to work it off. But no matter how much 'extra' there seems to be, it doesn't last longer than butter in a hot pan…

Can you describe the financial arrangements that you have?

Debra: I work full-time from home, which on a good week means about 30 hours a week, Sunday through Friday. We receive $1,200 in support to cover our rent and utilities.

What has been the most difficult aspect of having to transition from being a single twenty-four-year-old with minimal expenses to a married woman with financial responsibilities?

So many *expenses*! I mean, rent alone is insane! Money goes like water before you're even spending on things you *want* to spend on. I never had that before.

Do you factor "me" money into your budget? What about birthday presents and Chanukah gifts?

I love giving gifts. It's my thing. But I try to be smart about it, looking for something cute instead of expensive. I'll shop around or buy in the dollar store and write an adorable note, packaging the whole thing beautifully. (I keep ribbons when I get gifts, so I'm never short.) I'll also bake something if I have time – it's the thought that counts. But yeah, it ends up costing.

How does the reality of being supported measure up with your expectations?

I dreaded being supported. I hate knowing that my hardworking parents and in-laws are pressured to give me anything. I wish I could give *them*! I dream of the day when we'll be able to support ourselves without having to give them extra things to worry about – they give us so much already! My biggest dream? Making enough money to pay them back, so that they can relax a little, maybe even use it to support other siblings or things like that. I really wish I didn't have to take any money from them, but if I didn't, I'd be out on the street. And I can't work any harder or make any more money at this point.

Can you share a couple of examples of specific financial difficulties that have arisen in the past few months?

Yeah. The car's "cluster" broke. Whatever that is. Now we're a couple of hundred smackers poorer and the CD player *still* doesn't work.

Insurance is insane. I picked the most expensive plan we can (barely) afford, asked all the right questions, and still got nailed with a $1,000 fee for a service I thought was covered. I broke down in tears on the phone with the representative and now I am praying that my appeal letter, er, *appeals* to their more gracious side. We shall see.

If you could have any one question answered regarding your finances, what would it be?

How is this supposed to work?! Seriously! And how does *anyone* do it when they have to pay tuition? Maybe I should homeschool my kids when they get old enough… or win the lottery. How do people afford normal health insurance?

Stage 2: The Growing Family

The following two mothers have taken time from their very busy days to give us a glimpse into their financial life and show us what works, what doesn't, and how they feel about it all.

Elisheva & Dave Gross

Profile

Age: 35 and 38
Years married: 15
Children: 5, ranging in age from 2 to 12 years
Occupation: Husband: Special education tutor, full day
Wife: Part-time office manager

Monthly salaries:

Husband: (fluctuates)	$5,500
Wife:	$2,500
Total:	**$8,000**

Monthly Expenses:

Rent:	$2,000
Food:	$1,400
Tuition:	$1,330
Daycare:	$1,110
Insurance for wife:	$480
Car insurance:	$378
Car lease:	$290
Con Ed:	$210
Bus:	$125
Insurance for children:	$90 (CHP)
Phone and internet:	$90
Cell phones:	$80
National Grid (gas):	$45
Child with special needs — tutoring and lessons:	$1,200
Total:	**$8,618**

Debt:

Friend:	$17,500
Family:	$4,000
Small loan:	$275

My husband worked as a day school teacher for years before making a career switch this year to a government job. The school still owes him $25,000 dollars for last year! Our debt was accrued over time when there was nothing to live off. We didn't live beyond our means, but it did add up and we were forced to borrow. Thank God, we don't carry any credit card balance, and we pay our monthly bills in full.

Savings:

None. All depleted due to a medical crisis. We hope that the $50,000 we laid out will come back one day. If it does, it will be divided to begin saving for our children's weddings, God willing.

As your children grew and started school, how did you incorporate tuition into your budget?

When our tuition obligations started, my husband and I sat down and made two crucial decisions:

1: We always pay day school tuition the way we pay rent — the first of the month, no matter what. As people who have been involved in the world of Jewish education, we've seen the devastating effects of parents not paying tuition. It's a ripple effect: I'm owed money, therefore I owe my grocer, and then he can't pay his child's tuition, and the teachers suffer.

2: For our children's Jewish education, there are no compromises. Money can't and won't be an issue if a child needs tutoring or mentoring. We don't ask for a tuition discount. I would be embarrassed to ask my grocer for a discount on eggs — I trust that his price is fair. Same with tuition.

Of all the expenses you face, which do you find most stressful?

My credit card bill! Over the course of the month I charge all utility, tuition and food bills, and then I wait for the money, which is rightfully mine, to come in. When it doesn't, I go nuts, but we usually pull through, thank God. We've had to borrow from time to time, which is horrible. I hate debt. I also worry about how we'll manage in general when I look at our budget and see that on paper we shouldn't be making it.

Who is in charge of paying the bills?

Ahhhh. In the beginning, it was me, but when the stress began killing me, my husband took over. I went bonkers! He bounced checks and did a messy job, but he got it done, whereas I could not. Now we divide it 50/50. I take care of actually paying the bills, but I often warn him about a bill coming due and that I need the money to somehow appear....

Do you have a weekly or monthly budget?

I've given up on budgeting for a while. I hope that as soon as my husband's job begins in September, we'll go back to it. The way I work things is that my salary check gets put into an envelope and I don't deposit it right away — I save it to pay for my insurance and rent. This way, I know I have the money set aside for both, and it isn't being spent on anything else. I deposit the check on the 28th of the month and make out the rent and insurance check right way for the first of the month. I'd love to do that with all our money: divide it into envelopes and only spend what's inside. But that would only work when I actually have the money!

Can you share your strategies for coping with financial stress?

My husband says: Pray, pray and pray. Oh, and then be proactive and take on whatever menial job is offered that will help keep us going. And then keep counting your blessings.

As for me, I spend! Seriously, when I know I'm in the throes of a debt crisis, I cope by spending. It's dangerous, and not something I encourage, but those are the moments when I finally have the urge to spend, no matter what the amount. I've gotten to know that dark side of me and have worked on it — mainly by pushing off the purchase until I'm reasonable enough to understand that this is not what I really want. I really don't want to be poorer!

If you could have any question answered regarding your finances, what would it be?

Since I can't lower my expenses significantly enough for it to make a difference, what can I do to raise my income? How can I cut food expenses?

Shira & Moshe Dubovsky

Profile

Age: 33
Years married: 11
Children: 6, ranging from newborn to age 10
Occupation: Husband: CPA full time
Wife: formerly a secretary in a doctor's office, and now home full time.

Monthly salaries

$10,600 from husband's job
$1,300 income from rent of small apartment we have downstairs
Total: $ 11,900

Monthly expenses

Expense	Amount
Mortgage	$3,200
Home Insurance	$250
Auto insurance	$310
Health Insurance Plan	
$1300 + $400 in copays =	$1,700
Food	$1,200 staple groceries
	$300 meats/chicken
	$200 fish

$100 approx a month in take out — every Thursday my husband takes the kids out for pizza and I take a break and cook for Shabbat.

Total:	$1800
Utilities:	
Phone:	$40
Gas:	$75
Electricity:	$200

Cell phone for my husband: $59
Total: $374

Car Expenses

My husband commutes quite a lot, doing CPA consulting for different companies out of state, and his car lease is paid for by the company. $350 monthly for gas and $50 monthly car wash. Total: $400

Daycare

None right now, thank God, since I'm home. It's tough but first of all, it saves us quite a bit and secondly, one of my reasons for quitting my job was to be home with my kids.

Tuition

3 boys: 500 each = $1500
2 girls: 400 each = $800
Building funds combined: $1,000
Total: $3,300

Clothing

I estimate that I spend about $2,800 annually on the kids combined, $1,000 on myself, and $500 on my husband.

Taxes:	$400
Cleaning Help:	$250
Total Annual Expenses:	$140,970
Total income:	$142,800

Debt

None, thank God. Whatever we put on the credit card is paid by the end of the month. My in-laws live a frugal lifestyle and were able to pay for my husband's schooling. They also helped us with rent and other basic expenses while he went to school, so that helped a lot. It prevented us from falling into debt like others that I know did.

Savings: $6,000

We depleted our savings when we bought our house, but for the last year or so I've managed to put away $500 monthly — not a lot, and I'd like to put away more, but it's a start. We're saving towards bar mitzvahs and weddings, and eventually we'd like to put away some money so we can go on vacation every once in a while. So far, that's a luxury I can't afford. I also would love to have a retirement fund.

Do you have a weekly budget? How do you incorporate the costs of holidays and summertime into your expenses?

I have a monthly budget that covers the recurring expenses. I have an annual budget that I try not to exceed for expenses like clothing and holiday costs. I deduct that money every week so that when I need more before holidays, it's okay, and then for the next couple of months I know I need to lay low. In fact, we keep spreadsheets of all our expenses and compare them after the holiday is over to see how we can do better next time and why.

If you could have a question answered regarding your finances, what would it be?

1: How do you stop yourself from spending when you see a "good buy"? I can't seem to hold back when I see a great bargain, and the small things add up.

2: Is there a work-from-home job, not too many hours, that's lucrative? I would like to do something in the evenings for a few hours and have money to put away.

Your financial profile seems to present a rosier picture than others we have interviewed. Do you have financial stress in your life?

Since my husband is a CPA, I have a different kind of stress. In general, he works a 45-hour work week, 8 a.m. to 6 p.m. Monday through Thursday, and 9 a.m. to 2 p.m. on Friday. Pesach is my husband's craziest season, and I don't get any help at all from him. Sometimes I resent his being busy but then I remind myself that I'm the one who wants this lifestyle and I can't have it both ways.

I know that some people reading this may say, "What stress?! She's paying her bills, her husband makes a good living, and she's not working." I really agreed to this interview so that I could enlighten others. The assumption that someone like me does not have financial stress is both unfair and incorrect. I know that people look at me and say I totally can't relate to economic difficulties, but that's just not true. People need to understand that everyone has to live within her means, and for every person that presents her own, very real challenge. Less immediate, perhaps, but the stress and the challenge are there nonetheless.

Mesila Education Division

Core Values and Concepts

Some of the values and underlying ideas brought across by our curriculum are:

Bitachon and Hishtadlus

- **A believing Jew's attitude towards finance:** Striking the Torah-mandated balance between *bitachon* and *hishtadlus.*
- **Responsibility:** Realizing that the Torah obligates us to take reasonable measures to ensure our financial stability and future.

Financial Management

- **Awareness and control:** Meticulous recording of financial data brings an awareness and control, allowing us to make sensible decisions.
- **Planning ahead:** If you fail to plan, you plan to fail.
- **Paying attention to details:** Little things add up very quickly; attention to detail can make the difference between success and failure.

Responsibility to Others

- **Integrity:** Stringent honesty in money matters and in all areas, big and small.
- **Respecting property:** Accepting boundaries and respecting the property of others as well as our own.
- ***Chessed* and *tzedakah*:** Appreciating that our money is entrusted to us to share with others.
- **Positive peer pressure:** Recognizing that our actions impact what others will do and using that realization to trigger positive change.

Money and Materialism

- **Money is a means only:** Material gain is not an end in itself, but rather a tool to enable the effective implementation of Torah values.
- **Defining satisfaction:** Learning to identify satisfaction with values, relationships, and accomplishments, irrelevant of size of bank account.
- **Resisting materialism:** Learning to resist advertising lures and excessive emphasis on material goods.
- **Delayed gratification:** Waiting for things we really want brings emotional and material dividends.
- **Thinking independently:** What others have or need is not necessarily what I have or need – avoiding comparisons.

Prioritizing

- **Needs and wants:** Differentiating between needs and wants: Needs become stronger with time, while wants wane.
- **Balancing needs and wants:** Defining the financial goal as ensuring that we have everything we need and some of what we want.
- **Importance of prioritizing:** Ranking demands and desires and balancing time, energy, and money according to thought-out priorities.

Made in United States
Orlando, FL
04 November 2026

90200366R00128